KT-160-389

FRANCIS CLOSE HALL
LEARNING CENTRE
UNIVERSITY OF GLOUCESTERSHIRE
Swindon Road, Cheltenham GL50 4AZ
Tel: 01242 714600

Contents

3703939722

Writing Essays at University
A Guide For Students, By Students

Lin Norton & Edd Pitt
with Kathy Harrington
James Elander & Pete Reddy

UNIVERSITY OF
GLOUCESTERSHIRE
at Cheltenham and Gloucester

**FRANCIS CLOSE HALL
LEARNING CENTRE**

Swindon Road Cheltenham
Gloucestershire GL50 4AZ
Telephone: 01242 714600

WEEK LOAN

- 8 DEC 2009
- 1 OCT 2010
1 5 DEC 2010

WITHDRAWN

Write Now Centre for Excellence in Teaching & Learning

www.writenow.ac.uk/assessmentplus

Published April 2009 by
Write Now Centre for Excellence in Teaching & Learning
London Metropolitan University
Calcutta House, Old Castle Street
London EI 7NT

www.writenow.ac.uk/assessmentplus

Copyright © Write Now CETL 2009

All rights reserved. No part of this publication may be
reproduced, stored in a retrieval system, or transmitted,
in any form or by any means, electronic, mechanical,
photocopying, recording or otherwise, without the
prior permission of the copyright owner.

ISBN 978 0 9560695 0 4
A catalogue record for this book is available from
the British Library.

This book was also previously known by the title:
*What I Wish I Knew In My First Year About:
Writing Essays at University*

Design, illustration, typesetting
and editorial assistance by
Lionel@Openshaw.uk.net

Printed in the UK by Whitmont Press

4

Addressing (Answering) the Question

Introduction | Stick to the question like a very sticky thing! | Problems with interpreting the essay question | Breaking down the question | Referring back to the question | Tutors' views | Action Points

5

Structuring the Answer

Introduction | How to structure an essay | Start with the introduction | Planning your answer | Essay flow | Tutors' views | Action Points

6

Demonstrating Understanding

Introduction | Read, read, read... and then read some more! | Look at both sides of the argument | Understand what you are writing about | Tutors' views | Action Points

7

Developing Argument

Introduction | Appreciate both sides of the argument | Use of previous research | Avoiding bias | Links to other assessment criteria | Making your argument flow | Action Points

8

Use of Evidence

Introduction | Supporting your points | Getting good information | The perils of using quotes | The importance of using journals | Referencing your sources accurately | Action Points | Quiz Three: Spot the referencing mistakes

Writing Essays and Other Assignments at University: What You Need To Know

Foreword

Welcome to this guide. It is intended to help you make the most of your time at university by helping you to understand the assessment system and avoid the pitfalls that sometimes hold students back or discourage them. Many students think when they start their degree, 'I don't think I'm clever enough to be here'; and, sometimes, having difficulties with assessed work can reinforce that view. This guide is written to help you prevent that situation happening to you.

Before you think, 'Oh no, not another study skills manual', let us assure you that this book is definitely not that. Instead, it is the distillation of the experience of many students who have gone before you and who are keen to share their experiences with you. It also has some perspectives from tutors so you get a rounded picture. In this book there are a number of general principles which will be of use to students in many different subjects, although it often refers to Psychology. In fact, Lorraine, the student whose diary excerpts appear below, is a case in point as she studied both Psychology and English. Lorraine was a highly motivated mature student who struggled through the first year in her English subjects, getting low C grades despite lots of effort, but who suddenly 'got what it was all about' three quarters of the way through her first year and then started getting A grades, particularly in Psychology.

At the time when Lorraine was a student, no guidance was given on the assessment system or criteria, so she picked up her knowledge of this gradually, on her way to what eventually turned out to be a first class degree, but the insights came slowly and sometimes painfully. She, like all the other students quoted in this book, has readily agreed to share her journey of realisation.

Lorraine's journal

25th October
I think I'd better be quite realistic and aim for Bs – higher Bs if at all possible. I shall be very disappointed if I get Cs. I also think that as every assignment counts, more effort should be put into every single assignment than even last year.

Lorraine picks up the story in her second year when the marks for every assignment counted towards her final degree classification.

25th November
Well, the first mark is in – experiment on vigilance – got 69%. I feel ambivalent about it – pleased because it's been marked by someone new so I can obviously satisfy more than one tutor and slightly disappointed because I'm sure that report would have qualified for an A on last year's standards. I suppose, on the other hand, one's standards should be higher in the second year so all in all perhaps I didn't do too badly.

Lorraine's realisation that standards go up from one year to the next is a significant insight.

6th December
Handed in the Blake essay to Mr W – glad to have it finished and off my chest. I feel quite pleased with it, not because it's brilliant – it most certainly isn't – but because it's all my own work. Having made all these notes from the critics, I then took hardly any notice of them, or at least I'd absorbed and wrote them down in my own words instead of cutting and pasting. It took a lot of effort – longer than I've spent on any single assignment this year so I hope it'll get a good mark. Anything more than a B would be unrealistic given my performance last year, but I hope at least it'll be a good B and shall be most disappointed if it's a C or worse.

This was the turning point for Lorraine in her English work, where she finally realised that what her English tutors were looking for was her own opinions founded on her reading and understanding of the critics, rather than simply parroting back in her essay what the critics had said.

3rd January
Very nice comment on my Blake essay – got 69%. Mr W said that Mr E would have given it an A, which is very nice to know.

Lorraine is building on and consolidating her understanding of what's required in essays and going through a period of testing out this new understanding and then seeing what marks she gets. Every good mark reinforces her belief that she is on the right track. In effect, she is working out for herself what the assessment criteria are.

Lorraine pays close attention to the feedback she gets and incorporates this into her strategy of acting on feedback to more clearly understand what is required and improve on her future essays.

1st February
Handed in my essay on visual perception. Was hopeful it was B+ standard but after hearing how people have got As and B++s my hopes have gone down. It'll be interesting to see though because it's written in the new format, ie. exclusively argued by me from facts I've marshalled out of my reading.

13th February
Got B++ for visual perception and was disappointed because there were a lot of As. I do agree though that the main weakness was that it wasn't broad enough...

21st November
Am enjoying the Conrad course but I was wondering today whether reading the critics is a handicap, ie. it stultifies your own thoughts. I'd been reading Tanner on 'Lord Jim' last night and I really felt less clear on the lecture today than if I'd just relied on my own appreciation. Perhaps then extra work in English isn't so much reading the critics as thoroughly knowing the text, perhaps other texts by the same author and thinking.

The more I do think about it, the more convinced I am that what is needed is evidence of your own thinking critically applied to whatever information you've been given, be it Psychology or English or whatever. I should have it engraved on my heart – for every minute spent reading or learning or memorising, spend ten minutes THINKING. *And the nice thing about it is, the more you do think, the easier thinking becomes and if I can go into the exams without worrying too much about facts and figures (three years constant effort should hopefully dredge it up from somewhere) and concentrate on presenting thoughtful, critical yet constructive evaluations for answers, I should do better than if I seek to parade what little knowledge I may have acquired. I'll have to keep reminding myself though and in a way I think keeping this diary helps because it makes me stop and consider how I'm doing, where I've been going wrong, how I can improve etc. So the motto for the rest of this degree course is: 'Think, and when you think you can think no more, think again.'*

4th July
Had arranged with May to go up to College at about 2pm. While waiting nervously for Brian to arrive, the phone went about ten past one and it was Jane, who said she was at college and I'd got a first!! I kept saying 'are you sure, are you sure?'... I really can't believe it ... Was congratulated by all the staff. Found it all a bit overwhelming but very pleasing. I DID IT!!!

This unusually long entry is presented in its entirety as this is another major insight. Although she did not realise it at the time, what Lorraine was doing was taking a deep approach to her studies. Taking a deep approach means concentrating on understanding rather than memorising, relating new knowledge to what is already known, thinking independently and seeing things differently.

Lorraine didn't look back from this point and graduated with a first class combined honours degree in Psychology and English. Her final diary entry says it all.

Clearly, not every student will want to be like Lorraine, but a lot of what she says in her study diary is relevant to anyone starting who wants to do their best at university and get good grades in their written assignments.

Note to readers: how to use this book

The authors of this book and the students we interviewed, who have so generously given up their time to talk about their own understandings of what is involved in being assessed, all hope that this small guide will help to make your own experience of assessment in Higher Education that little bit easier.

We have included some activities and exercises which should be fun to do as well as help you understand the 'system' a little better. At the end of each chapter you will see some suggested Action Points which will help you make the best use of this guide by showing you how to apply what you have read to your own work.

You can dip into this book and read it in any order you like, but if you need immediate guidance on the assessment criteria that we have described as 'core' criteria, go directly to Chapters Four – Nine.

Another strategy you might like is to concentrate first on reading all the quotes from both the students and the tutors. In the following chapters all quotes are in *italic* type in the outermost columns, so you can pick them out easily. Where possible the quotes are placed alongside the relevant part of the main text that refers to them. (As you read the main text you will also usually find a cue when to refer to the relevant quote.) Students' views are signalled by a blue dotted line above them and staff views are signalled by a black dotted line above them. While we have kept to the essential meaning of what has been said, some of the quotes have been changed slightly to make them easier to read. 'Running headings' at the top right of each double page spread (such as 'What you need to know' on the page opposite) serve as a reminder of which chapter you are reading and help to navigate your way through the book.

....

JAN, STUDENT

*"Quotes from students look like this, with a **blue** dotted line."*

....

JOHN, TUTOR

*"Quotes from staff look like this, with a **black** dotted line."*

How Assessment Aware Are You?

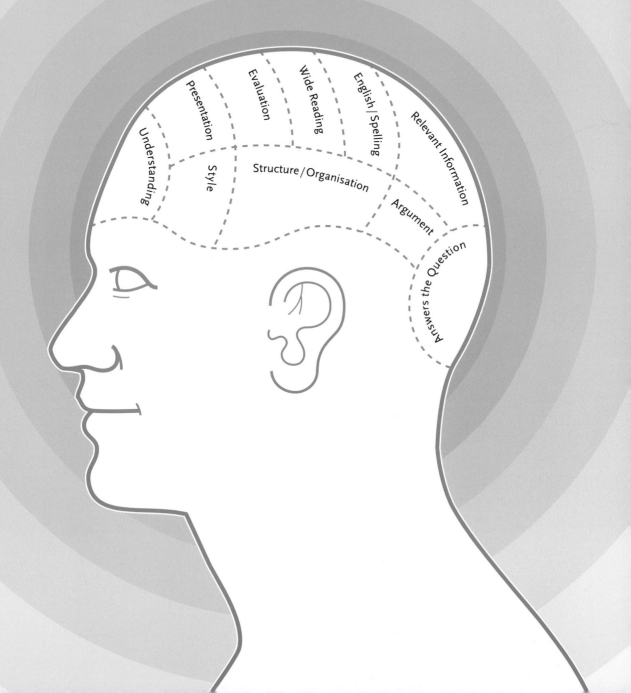

Understanding · Presentation · Evaluation · Wide Reading · English / Spelling · Relevant Information · Style · Structure / Organisation · Argument · Answers the Question

Chapter One
How Assessment Aware Are You?

We believe that you will save yourself a lot of time, and potentially some disappointment in your own progress, if you begin your studies at university by becoming aware of the assessment system, how it works and how you can make it work for you. This is not intended to be a cynical exercise; rather it is intended to alert you to how assessment works in most university courses. By realising how the system works, you will be able to take control and empower yourself as an effective learner and a successful student.

See the facing page to find out how assessment aware you are about essays. Here are some statements that students and staff express about essays and assessment. Read each one and then place a tick in the appropriate column headed either 'True' or 'False'. Answers are on page 110 and your score interpretation is on page 115.

Once you have found out how knowledgeable you are about assessment in general, we would like you to see how much you know about assessment criteria. But first, a word or two of explanation is needed.

1

Quiz One: Your assessment awareness   True — *or* — False?

1 | The marks you get for an essay range from 0 – 100.   ....

2 | A pass mark is always 50%.   ....

3 | If you fail an assignment in your first year, this will affect your final degree.   ....

4 | Tutors vary in what they expect of you in written essays.   ....

5 | It's important to write in as elaborate a style as you can.   ....

6 | Handing in an essay before it's due will impress your tutor, who will give you a higher mark.   ....

7 | Exceeding the word limit and using big words or technical jargon will get you higher marks.   ....

8 | Students in their first year do not generally understand what assessment criteria are.   ....

9 | Tutors sometimes give new students higher marks than their work deserves – to encourage them.   ....

10 | Tutors reward ability more than effort.   ....

11 | Most students think essays are the fairest form of assessment.   ....

12 | A really good student can complete a top-class essay in one sitting.   ....

Now go to pages 110 – 115 for answers and associated advice.

Criterion and criteria: what is the difference?

Before we get into a detailed discussion, let us just explain a little about the use of the word 'criteria', which is the plural form of the word 'criterion'. According to the Chambers Twentieth Century Dictionary, 'criterion' is a noun, which is defined as 'a means or standard of judging'. When tutors talk about assessment, they rarely use the singular noun; more often they refer to the plural: 'criteria'.

What are assessment criteria?

Although we never use the term in our ordinary, everyday lives, we use assessment criteria all the time, such as when we are shopping for a new pair of trainers. Are we looking for a brand name, a design, colour, style or how well they seem to fit the purpose for which we want to use them? Do we want them for walking, tennis, football, etc? In deciding whether or not to buy the trainers, we make a judgment based on all these factors. The 'factors' are, in effect, assessment criteria. This is exactly what tutors do when they mark your written work; only in this case the assessment criteria are devised to help them judge how well you have learned the subject on which you are being assessed.

Which are the most important assessment criteria?

This next quiz is designed to see how much you know about the assessment criteria that Psychology tutors use when marking essays.

Quiz Two: Ranking assessment criteria

Look at the following list of assessment criteria, which were identified by six Psychology tutors in a study by Norton (1990), and put them in order of importance, where 1 is the most important and 9 the least important. Then tick those assessment criteria that you believe are 'core' criteria, ie. those that all tutors would recognise as referring to important features of a good essay.

Rank : 1 – 9	Assessment criteria	Core criterion?
....	Understanding	....
....	Wide reading	....
....	English / Spelling	....
....	Relevant information	....
....	Answers the question	....
....	Evaluation	....
....	Presentation / Style	....
....	Argument	....
....	Structure / Organisation	....

So how did you do?
Go to pages 116 – 120 for the answers and explanation.

Chapter Two
**The Assessment System:
How It Works and
How You Can Make It
Work For You**

Chapter Two
The Assessment System: How It Works and How You Can Make It Work For You

2

Introduction

The assessment system is often an area that students find one of the most difficult to get to grips with. Many of you have come straight to university from school and you are used to your teacher telling you exactly what is going to happen and where you can find information related to your subject. Even in work settings, you were probably told quite clearly what to do. University life is different; an emphasis is placed on you developing your independent research skills and learning to help yourself. You might be asking yourself the question, 'So why do I need to know about the assessment system?'. A number of graduating students that we talked to have commented that they wished they knew then what they know now. With this in mind, this chapter will give you some helpful hints on what to look for and what to do in order to make the assessment system work for you.

Why is it important to work out the assessment system?

At the beginning of a module you are given an outline of how the module will be structured; important details such as examination and coursework deadlines are usually communicated to you. However, many students take this information at face value and don't consider what it is exactly that tutors are looking for in their work. This is a potential 'disaster' just waiting to happen. Unlike school where the examination boards and examiners are not your teachers, in the university system, the tutors who teach you are the same people who design the module, the learning aims and the assessment system. Most importantly of all, your tutors are the people who will be marking your work. So to turn a potential 'disaster' into a triumph, you need to realise that there is nothing magical or mystical going on that is outside your control.

The assessment system is a process that you can become pro-active in by finding out:
- what tutors are actually looking for in your assignments
- why they think it is important

Raising your awareness of the system in this way will give you a head start not just in terms of your assignments, but also in understanding what studying and learning at university level is all about. There are many debates about what university students should be able to do, but one of the most helpful ways of describing it is in Stephenson's (1988) definition of 'capability'.

Thinking about this definition, you can immediately see that Higher Education is about encouraging you to stand on your own two feet, to become confident in what you do and why you do it. Psychology assignments typically encourage you to become more confident in finding evidence, evaluating its persuasiveness and using it to formulate your own ideas and arguments about a topic.

How do I find out what my tutors are looking for?

The question of what your tutors want can be tackled in many different ways. What we have tried to do in this book is to let as many students as possible tell you about what they have found out about assessment from their own personal experience. We have gathered this information through interviews and focus groups. The Psychology students who took part have willingly allowed us to use their words in the hope that what they have learned about assessment will help you. We have also carried out a number of interviews with Psychology tutors in order to present as rounded a picture as possible. Here are some of the things that students have said about what they did to find out what was expected of them.

"... an integration of knowledge, skills, personal qualities and understanding used appropriately and effectively... Capability can be observed when we see people with justified confidence in their ability to take effective and appropriate action; explain what they are about ... and continue to learn from their experiences as individuals and in association with others, in a diverse and changing society."

Requesting feedback on a draft

Jane is a first-year Psychology student who was quite confused about what was required. As Jane says, she didn't understand what her tutor was looking for so she adopted the strategy of handing the essay in early for her tutor to comment on. Many students think that tutors do not want to spend time with them outside the teaching sessions; however, most tutors are perfectly happy to do this. Arranging to see your tutor with a draft essay shows that you have gone away and researched your area and you want to know what to do to write a good essay.

However, a word of caution here; if you want to hand your essay in early, make sure you give your tutors sufficient time to look over it. You can't give it to them the day before it's due and expect them to drop everything and have a look at it instantly. They are busy people, too!

Asking for advice on a plan

Another useful strategy mentioned by a number of students we interviewed was to do a plan of the essay and ask the tutor what she or he thinks. This helps as the tutor can then clarify if the student is looking at the right areas and is actually answering the question. This is a good strategy to adopt as it only takes a few moments to catch the tutor after a lecture and she or he can give you some advice about your plan. Most tutors do not mind you asking them for this type of advice. Going to see them when you don't understand something is all part of your development both personally and academically.

Using the module handbook

The module handbook is usually given out at the beginning of a module or is made available electronically. It is designed to give an outline of the whole module and tell

JANE, 1ST-YEAR PSYCHOLOGY
"They have given you this area and they are looking for certain standards that you've got to meet. To be honest I didn't know what the marker was looking for. In fact what I did one time was to finish an essay early and hand it in to him to have a look at."

RASHID, 3RD-YEAR STUDENT, SOUGHT HIS TUTORS' ADVICE
"In one of my first lectures a tutor said to us don't go and ask the tutors anything as they are too busy doing their own research, and I thought well what are we going to do if we need help? I ignored this and went to see some of my tutors and they told me what to do. Some are more helpful than others. I guess it's swings and roundabouts."

you what the tutors are looking for. As Karen points out, if she doesn't understand something in the module handbook, then she makes a point of going to the module tutors to ask them what it means.

Don't be put off!

Of course, it must be said that tutors are fallible human beings like the rest of us, so occasionally you will be brushed off or turned away by an individual. This may be because it was a bad time you chose, or that the tutor concerned was facing other pressures. However, it is very rare indeed that with a bit of negotiation and common courtesy a tutor would refuse to help you at all.

Attending everything

This may seem obvious, but in fact many students are not as careful as they should be about attending absolutely everything that is on their course. There are always plenty of good excuses not to go to that 9.00 am lecture, especially if your best friend has said she'll take notes for you. Someone else's recall of a session fits in with their perceptions and understanding, not yours, so the sad fact is, other people's notes are rarely helpful. You should make every effort not to miss out, no matter how unpromising or boring the class session might sound. Getting someone to sign you in, which is what some students do, is not a good idea as although you get a tick for attendance, you may miss vital gems of information that could help you get a better grade. Many tutors will give really useful tips and hints for essays and examinations in their lectures and seminars. Equally importantly, the more you attend, the better the understanding you will gain of the whole subject area.

KAREN, 2ND-YEAR STUDENT
"It's hard to know exactly what they want. Some tutors write what they want in the lectures, others don't, so it's a bit of a guessing game really. I often go and see them if I am unsure. The module handbook gives you an idea but it's not always that great if you don't understand."

SEAN, 1ST-YEAR STUDENT, EXPERIENCED HELPFULNESS
"He always told us where his office was and that he was available for us to go and see him. People have told me that you should at least go and speak to them if they make the time available as they could tell you lots and also it would show him that I made the effort."

SEAN ALSO REALISED THE IMPORTANCE OF ATTENDANCE IN HIS FIRST YEAR
"They give you an outline of the essay and what they tend to want you to write. Also going to the lectures you tend to be able to pick up what the tutors want."

Psychology tutors want evidence

"They are looking for journal articles supporting everything. Recent research."

MEENA, 3RD-YEAR STUDENT

"I think it was learning the research skills. I didn't know how to research really and you pick that up as you go along using the libraries and journals. In the first year I tended to get a lot of the information from books and also searching other areas like the internet. I was getting Cs. In the second and third year I started to go beyond that and use journals."

STEVEN, 3RD-YEAR STUDENT

"They want you to show that you understand the material and that you know what you're talking about. Wider reading as well, show that we don't only read the handouts. They give you the bare bones and you have to put the meat on them. They want you to show that you have researched the area thoroughly and that you have spent time and effort in putting your essay together."

At university, examinations and essays are the main ways of assessing what students have learned, and Psychology is no exception. Many students struggle to make the transition from school writing styles to university writing styles within the first year of study. One of the major stumbling blocks is that of evidence. At university, students need to write about what has happened before in the discipline, what people have found and how they found it. The tutors at university expect you to write about previous research and show that you have researched the assignment topic through reading journals and books. Many students know that this is what their tutors are looking for.

The gathering of information for essays is a skill that you will develop throughout your time at university. This skill is essential as it increases not only your understanding of the topic area but also the depth that your essays convey, and this has a direct relationship with how well you eventually do in your modules. Meena's experience is important for it shows the value that Psychology places on journal information. As soon as she realised this, her grades started to improve.

Talking to Steven, another third-year student who has experienced both 'good and bad' in his three years, we can see how he has developed a good understanding of what his tutors are looking for.

Both Meena and Steven have learned about the importance of reading and researching in preparation for their essays. If you want to read more now about how to use such evidence in your essays, go to Chapter Eight.

Why do I need to know about assessment criteria?

Many students begin their undergraduate degree by being unaware of the assessment criteria. Steven explains why ignoring the criteria is a mistake.

Students have had many mixed experiences with understanding assessment criteria and with not realising how important they are. Many have reported that at the beginning of their course they were either unaware of them or they chose to ignore them, believing that they knew better.

James learnt a valuable but very hard lesson. He failed a year, and reflecting on this, he thinks that it was probably due to not following the assessment criteria. The transition from school to university and the difference between the ways students are taught is demonstrated by David's experience of assessment criteria.

David's experience is a useful lesson, as it is a very common perception by new students that they will be 'spoon fed' all the information they need. However, this is not what university education is about, and from the very first lecture you will be expected to take responsibility for your own learning. Both James and David are really good examples of what happens when you don't realise the importance of taking account of the assessment criteria for assignments. If you adapt to using the assessment criteria from the start, then you are giving yourself a good chance of getting the best marks that you can in each module. In the next chapter we will be exploring how assessment criteria are used in the marking process.

STEVEN, 3RD-YEAR STUDENT
"Well, I look at the module guide, which tells me the assessment criteria. If you don't follow these criteria then you are in big trouble. They're there as a framework in which to base your answer."

JAMES COMMENTS ON HIS EXPERIENCE
"I used to not really look at the assessment criteria and wonder what the tutor was looking for, but as I have progressed through the years I have realised that if you don't follow what they ask, then you tend not to do very well. That's probably why I failed my first year."

DAVID, 3RD-YEAR STUDENT
"In the first year I didn't really utilise the assessment criteria and therefore I didn't know what the tutors were looking for. It seems silly now not to look at the assessment criteria, but I guess in the first year I just took it for granted that I would be told everything without having to actually do any independent thinking."

The Assessment System: How It Works and How You Can Make It Work For You
Action Points

→ Take control and find out what the assessment system is for each of your modules.

→ Ask tutors for help with your written work, but be well prepared (ie. bring with you a draft essay, plan or the module handbook).

→ Understand the particular importance of evidence and research in Psychology work.

→ Start using journals when researching for your essays (although not strictly required in your first year, the sooner you get to grips with these, the better your assignments will be).

→ Realise how important assessment criteria are and resolve to find out what they are for each assignment you are given.

NSWERING THE QUESTION
TRUCTURING THE ESSAY
EMONSTRATING
NDERSTANDING
SING EVIDENCE
EVELOPING ARGUMENT
VALUATING SOURCES
SE OF WRITTEN LANGUAGE

Chapter Three
**Assessment Criteria
and the
Marking Process**

Chapter Three
Assessment Criteria and the Marking Process

Introduction

Getting to grips with the assessment system very early on in your university life will be advantageous to your progression towards that final graduation day. In the previous chapter we looked at why it's important to work out the assessment system and how you can make this system work for you. This chapter takes you one step further and explains what assessment criteria are, how you can identify them and what your tutors mean by them. One of the keys to success is to know what the people marking your work consider important and then to concentrate on getting these things right.

The assessment criteria for any given assignment are a list of specific aspects that tutors look for when they are marking your work, and they will be judging how well you demonstrate each of these aspects. Assessment criteria can vary from subject to subject and from task to task, but most tutors would agree that the basic core assessment criteria for essay writing include the following (also see the answers to Quiz Two on page 116):

• answering the question
• structuring the essay
• demonstrating understanding
• developing an argument
• using evidence
• evaluating sources
• use of written language

It is important for you to understand each one of these criteria so that you write a balanced essay in which all the criteria are met to the best of your ability. This maximises your chances of achieving the best grade possible.

Students' understandings of assessment criteria

As we mentioned earlier, when asked what assessment criteria are, many first-year students are unsure. This may be due to a number of reasons, such as, they didn't know where to find them, or they didn't have them at school so were not aware that they needed to know about them at university. However, some students were more clued in.

These quotes show that these students know that the assessment criteria are what your tutors are going to assess you on. This point cannot be emphasised enough. Many students have realised, unfortunately sometimes too late, that if they do not follow the criteria, they will not do very well.

Paul's thoughts are very typical of many students and echo those of Steven, James and David in Chapter Two. Although Paul had an idea of what the assessment criteria were, he still did not look at them in his first year. However, he now realises that they are important, and he uses them as a tool to help keep him informed of what he is doing throughout an essay and to keep him on the right track.

Where to find assessment criteria

Assessment criteria are often found in quite different places. When we asked students where they first heard of them or found them, we had many different responses, as the following excerpts from a focus group discussion show. This probably goes some way to explain why first-year students can sometimes have so much trouble in knowing exactly what they are and where to find them. Phillip, a first-year student in the focus group, explains overleaf a few different methods of finding out where they are and what they are:

"Assessment criteria are a set of standards that you have to adhere to, to get a certain grade."

"It's a document that they use to distinguish how they are going to assess you."

PAUL, 2ND-YEAR STUDENT, EXPLAINS HIS EXPERIENCE OF ASSESSMENT CRITERIA AND WHAT IT MEANS TO HIM

"Isn't that the criteria that the tutors judge your essays on? Don't they have to stick to them so that they can grade your essays? I think they might use them as a guide or maybe they know them so well they just know what to do. I never used to look at them in the first year but now I have realised that it is essential to look at them while I am doing my essays just so that I know that I am on the right track and know what I'm doing."

PHILLIP, 1ST-YEAR STUDENT
"It might be posted on the web, or told to you by your tutor in a session. You are going to be assessed in an essay at the end and you are probably told that, ideally at the beginning of the course. I look on the web."

PAULA, 1ST-YEAR STUDENT
"They put criteria on the back of the submission sheet – like a table, don't they? It's got grades and they tick each box, like 'presentation' for example."

JULIE, 3RD-YEAR STUDENT, DOESN'T LIKE THIS PRACTICE
"I don't think it is a good idea to put it on the back of the sheet that you are using to submit your essay. You have already written your essay so you might not have looked at the submission sheet until you hand it in."

FEMI, 2ND-YEAR STUDENT, USES ONLINE SOURCES
"I always look on the website. Tutors normally put the question on there and then a little piece about what they want done, like pointers."

Interestingly, a debate then ensued about the fact that the assessment criteria can be found on some assignment submission sheets. Our advice is to make sure you know where to get the assessment criteria before you submit your essay. If you actually get your submission sheet at the time you are writing your essay, then it is fine to use it as a way of knowing what the assessment criteria are. However, if the criteria are not on the submission sheet, you need to find out where they are. Some students, such as Femi, use electronic sources instead.

He gives a good piece of advice, as he explains that tutors sometimes give little pointers of what they are looking for, which means that if you have a look at the website, you might get some extra help. As we have said before, it is worth remembering that it is the tutor who will be marking your work, not some faceless external person, so if you know what your tutor specifically wants, then that has to give you an advantage.

The final source for criteria, and possibly the easiest to access, is the module handbook itself. These handbooks vary in size and quality, but they tend to have similar information in common: they contain the module aims, learning outcomes and assessment criteria for that particular module. As well as having all the information about the module, most of them also break down the assessment criteria and give you pointers on what to do in your essays in relation to the assessment criteria.

What do the assessment criteria measure?

The assessment system at university means that simple right and wrong answers are rarely part of what is expected in students' work, unless they are multiple choice question tests. Therefore, the tutor marking an essay is faced with many different possible answers to any one specific essay title. In order for the tutor to mark students' work effectively, she or he needs to have assessment criteria to give an overall grade. Obviously the grade at the end is what students are primarily concerned with; but how does the tutor reach the decision to award this grade? Sarah's comments show that she understands the role played by criteria in the marking process.

Both Sarah and Asif's quotes show they have realised that assessment criteria are used to measure their learning in the subject area. This is an important point to remember. You need to show the tutor that you have learnt and understood what you are writing about. This is even more important in the final year of study, as tutors will be looking for far deeper answers that demonstrate an excellent level of understanding and application of knowledge acquired during your time in Higher Education. Assessment criteria are, therefore, not only tools tutors use to mark your work, but also a set of indicators for you that will help you write better essays.

What do tutors expect from first-year students?

The transition into Higher Education can be difficult for many first-year students, so if you're finding it hard, you're not alone! Part of the problem in adjusting to this new level of education is trying to work out what your tutors expect of you, and this can become quite stressful when you have to hand in a piece of work that is going to be assessed. Knowing what tutors expect from the first-year is a genuine advantage for the new student. One of the first things you should remember is that it is expected that you will learn as you go along. In virtually all universities, how you perform in the first year will not affect your final degree classification, which gives you the chance to learn from taking risks with new ways of

PENNY, 2ND-YEAR STUDENT, EXPLAINS WHERE SHE FINDS ASSESSMENT CRITERIA
"I always go straight to the module handbook and I have done that since day one. The module handbook is really good for pointers and information about what to do. I don't really use the website as I prefer it in print, in my hand."

SARAH UNDERSTANDS THE ROLE OF CRITERIA IN THE MARKING PROCESS
"Assessment is a way of finding out if a student has learnt what you wanted them to learn and those criteria will supposedly evaluate whether that learning has or hasn't taken place. Whether or not it is always effective is a different question, but that is what it is there for – to see if learning has actually taken place."

ASIF, 1ST-YEAR STUDENT
"Assessment criteria are your learning outcomes from your course, whether it is assignment based or exam based, and what you have to fulfil to get the required grade."

"At first-year level I think students are struggling with joining the 'Psychology Club', learning the terminology, the way psychologists think and speak and do things. I think that our students, particularly, are in a difficult position because they have to do combined honours, so there's a whole thing of using different voices, different styles, different registers for the different subjects. If you give students feedback and say, 'you need to develop your argument' or 'you need to structure your argument better', then I don't think they know what that means. I think that an essay title is such an artificial thing, it's so dependent on the subject. Those words there [on the sheet] mean something quite simple to us because we live in that culture, but they don't mean anything to students because they're not in that culture."

learning and writing and, importantly, from making mistakes. Having read what students think about assessment criteria, let's now look at what their tutors have to say.

Lena, a senior tutor in Psychology and a researcher in essay writing, made the following comment when asked why she thought first-year students did not understand what was meant by assessment criteria.

Ken's point [on facing page] highlights the problem students have when they try to cling to ways of doing things that worked well for them in previous study, such as at A Level. As he says, students who adopt this strategy will find it only works for a short while. Successful university students are those who are prepared to give up old ways of writing in favour of developing new ones which are well adapted to the demands of the new educational context.

Progression

This is something that many tutors talked about when asked what they thought about students' understanding of assessment criteria – how students' writing improved with experience.

Francis makes the point overleaf that students do not always understand the importance of assessment criteria and so do not act on the feedback they are given.

Both Colin [facing page] and Francis [overleaf] are saying the same thing: students do not always understand what their tutors mean when they give feedback in relation to assessment criteria. This is another indication that the earlier that you can understand the assessment criteria and show this understanding in your essay writing, the better you will do.

Which criteria do tutors think are the most important when marking students' essays?

The tutors we interviewed expressed different opinions about this question. Looking at their answers will show you why you need to make sure that your understanding matches that of the tutor who will be marking your work.

Addressing the question

Addressing the question may sound very simple and obvious for many students. The common school of thought amongst students is that 'obviously, I am addressing the question if I am answering it'.

Roger's quote overleaf shows very clearly an important difference between students' and tutors' interpretations of what addressing the question means. Time and again, inexperienced undergraduates take this to mean that they should write down all they know about a topic, but tutors are very clear that this is a bad strategy and almost certainly means they are not addressing the question. The skill, and this is something that you will develop over the duration of your course, is to read around the topic and try to apply relevant parts of what you find directly to the question. A tip is to look at every single paragraph you write and ask yourself 'Is this paragraph answering the question?' If the answer is 'yes', leave it in, if 'no', get rid of it!

Understanding and developing an argument

While all tutors agreed that addressing the question is the single most important thing a student must do in completing an essay assignment, there are differences in how much weight individual tutors give to the other criteria. Narinder, for example, puts demonstrating understanding and developing an argument at the top of her list.

KEN, SENIOR TUTOR OF 15 YEARS' EXPERIENCE
"Some students don't have a clue. Part of the problem is with people who have some understanding from A Level that's often extremely pedantic and rigid. They'll come here and, it's sad really, because it works out well for them to begin with, and at the end of the first year people who've been trying to adapt to the Higher Education style can develop, but others don't develop at all."

DAVE, SENIOR TUTOR
"Students do get noticeably better as they progress through the course. At A Level they are slightly molly-coddled and don't really think about criteria."

COLIN, TUTOR
"Students' writing improves with experience. Generally you get better essays in the final year than in the first year. So, in some ways they must have picked up what we mean."

FRANCIS, TUTOR, THINKS
STUDENTS DO NOT ALWAYS
UNDERSTAND THE
IMPORTANCE OF CRITERIA

"It takes a while. There's a noticeable progression through the course and clearly some criteria are less well understood because with essays you're having to constantly make the same comments. And they still make the same omissions or errors even when they get feedback."

ROGER, TUTOR, EXPLAINS
THE IMPORTANCE OF
ADDRESSING THE QUESTION

"This is very important, I do insist on the question that I asked being answered. People are more likely to fail or do badly if they just write everything they know about a topic and don't focus on the question."

Helping students become independent learners is one of the fundamental goals of Higher Education, and although all tutors will value this goal, they will have differing ideas about which assessment criteria are most closely linked to achieving it. Some tutors, for example, will regard being able to critically evaluate as key to becoming an independent learner; whereas others, like Narinder [facing page], think first of the ability to demonstrate one's understanding and develop an argument. In truth, all of the criteria are relevant to becoming an independent learner, and studying at university is an opportunity for you to develop skills that will not only help you do well in your studies but also prepare you for the world of employment, therefore if you can demonstrate that you are an independent learner this will benefit your future career aspirations as well as help you do well in your studies.

However, although all of the assessment criteria are relevant to your success, it is worthwhile trying to discover which of the criteria the tutor marking your work regards as most important for the particular assignment you are working on, as this will allow you to produce an answer which takes into account the specific way your work will be assessed.

Achieving a higher grade

Students often ask how they can get a better grade. Many students find they keep getting the same grades throughout their second and third year and they wonder why it is they can't make that jump to the higher bracket.

What Jonathon is saying [facing page] is that all the other assessment criteria should be followed, but, in his view, the one that is crucial to achieving higher grades is the criterion of critical evaluation. Meeting this criterion is something that is quite difficult to do in the first year, but any attempt to do it will pay dividends and be a good preparation for the demands of second- and third-year study.

So far in this book, we have concentrated on a general discussion about assessment; in the following chapters (Four – Nine), we are going to take a very detailed look at each of the core assessment criteria.

NARINDER, TUTOR, EXPLAINS SOME DIFFERENCES IN HOW TUTORS PRIORITISE CRITERIA
"Understanding and developing the argument are more important for me personally because they are key to the student being able to go off and be an independent learner."

JONATHON, SENIOR TUTOR, EXPLAINS HOW STUDENTS CAN MAKE THE JUMP UPWARDS IN THEIR GRADES
"What's more important is evaluating and critically evaluating, because that would take someone from a lower grade to a top grade."

Assessment Criteria and the Marking Process
Action Points

→ Develop a good understanding of what assessment criteria are and what part they play in the essay grades you get.

→ Make sure you know where to find them for each of your modules.

Chapter Four
Answering the Question

Chapter Four
Addressing (Answering) the Question

Introduction

Addressing the question is the main objective of an essay assignment, and how well you can do this has a direct relationship to the grade you will get for both coursework and examination essays. However, many first-year students do not understand sufficiently what the question is asking them to do, and they opt instead for writing generally about the topic area. This chapter takes a look at the views of many students about what addressing the question means to them. It also looks at the tutors' views and what advice they offer to give you a better understanding of why it is crucial to understand what essay questions are actually asking you to do.

Stick to the question like a very sticky thing!

A common misconception among students, and first-year students in particular, is to look at the question and take what it says at face value. The problem with this approach is that such answers merely 'scratch the surface' and often discuss generally, rather than in any detail, the specific areas mentioned in the question.

All of these examples from the students identify the need for you to stick to what the question is asking and not to digress from that. A good point to remember is that 'waffle will not get you marks'.

The issue of just scratching the surface in essays is a real concern of many university tutors. To get higher marks in an essay, therefore, you have to look at the question and really think about what it is asking you to do. Paul, a third-year student, comments on what he used to do and how he has now realised that such a strategy would not get very good marks.

Problems with interpreting the essay question

Interpretation of the essay title can be confusing at university level. How one person interprets a question may be completely different to that of another person. This can be quite a difficult problem for inexperienced students to overcome. Chris, a first-year student, comments on this below.

As he says, he struggles with this, and he is not the only one to feel this way. To help you avoid getting stuck like this, it can be helpful to ask yourself: 'From what angle am I going to attack this question? What is my stance on the issues in the question?' Once you have made your mind up, you can then think about answering the question. A useful tip is to use the introduction to state how you interpret the question and how you intend to address it in the essay. By doing this, the tutor knows you have not gone off at a tangent but have genuinely interpreted the question in a different way from how she or he might have understood it.

Breaking down the question

Breaking down the question into small manageable chunks could alleviate the problems with interpretation that many students face. A good piece of advice is to look at the question in sections.

Many essay questions are easy to break down as they are often designed to ask you more than one specific question. For example, they might ask you to evaluate a theory and then discuss its impact on the subject or topic area. If you were to break the question down, you would firstly evaluate the theory itself, offering positive and negative points about it, and then go on to address the part of the question that asks you to discuss the impact of the theory on the subject.

PAUL, 3RD-YEAR STUDENT, ON WHAT ADDRESSING THE QUESTION MEANS TO HIM
"Not digressing from what I have been asked to write about. I used to waffle and wander off the point, but now I stick to the question. If you don't do that properly you don't get the marks. Your writing must be relevant and answer the question rather than talking about something for the sake of it."

JACK, 3RD-YEAR STUDENT
"You need to see beyond the question and really try to know what you're talking about. It's easy to get carried away with answering the question as you think and then not actually answering it."

CHRIS, 1ST-YEAR STUDENT
"I don't think it's that simple. One person might read the question quite differently to another and what do you put a stronger emphasis on? I struggle with answering the question sometimes."

Referring back to the question

The advice offered about interpreting and breaking down the question will help you gain good marks; however, you also have to remember that at all times you must refer what you are writing about back to the question. This will stop you simply writing all you know about a particular topic, which as mentioned earlier does not constitute addressing the question. The skill is to find relevant information and then use it to answer the question.

Janet's comments are useful. There is always a strong temptation to use all your research and reading, even when it is not completely relevant, in the hope that it will impress your tutor and get you a high mark. It won't! The sad fact is that you have to be ruthless and prune out all irrelevant material, no matter how hard you have worked on finding it.

PAUL'S IDEAS
MAKE VERY GOOD SENSE
"Sometimes you may actually be answering the question in a completely different way to what is required. The best way is to break the question down into parts and try to think, 'What do they want me to say here? Which angle do I attack this question from?' And then set about strictly sticking to that plan and not wavering away from it.

JANET SHARES
HER EXPERIENCES
"Essay titles are usually split into one or two sentences. Look at each section of the question and focus on what they actually want from you, always referring back to the question, rather than going off at a tangent or writing about what you have found in literature reviews or old books that are not necessarily linked to the question."

Tutors' views on addressing the question

The views that students hold about addressing the question do not always match up with what happens when they actually write their essays. Speaking to tutors has revealed many different areas where they feel their students could improve. They also have some useful advice on how to actually address the question.

Martin makes a crucial distinction which so often trips up students. This is that answering the question does not mean writing everything you know about a topic; instead, it means being selective and using what you do know to respond to what the essay question is asking you to do.

Tutors also reported that the issue of 'going off on a tangent' is a major problem with many students. This point is really important; if you go off on a tangent in your essay, you will be throwing away good marks.

Yasmin's advice overleaf ties in with the research that we carried out on 'Rules of the Game', where there was a common misconception by students that using long words and technical jargon would impress their tutors. The short answer is, it doesn't! Our advice is to keep your answers simple and to the point and do not try to 'jazz up' what you are trying to say by using irrelevant material. [Tutors' comments continued overleaf →]

MARTIN, SENIOR TUTOR, ON HOW ADDRESSING THE QUESTION AFFECTS GRADING
"This is very important; I do insist on the question that I asked being answered. People are more likely to fail or do badly if they just write everything they know about a topic and don't focus on the question. It's just that to me a 2:1 answers the question, but a 2:2 talks about the topic without necessarily answering the question."

JAMIE, TUTOR, HAS THIS TO SAY ON ADDRESSING THE QUESTION
"They look at the question and start off with an introduction and say this is what I'm going to answer, but then they wander off and talk about something entirely different. And then sometimes they say, 'in conclusion...' and they look at the question again – but quite often they don't even do that. Sometimes they conclude something that isn't actually within the question that you asked them."

YASMIN, SENIOR TUTOR
"Answer the question that I've asked you, provide me with the information that is relevant and not a load of irrelevant stuff. Make it as clear and coherent as you can without trying to be kind of clever about it. Sometimes students try to be, and I'm thinking particularly about undergraduates here, but they try to wrap things up and make it more sophisticated than it needs to be, and then they get themselves lost in using words and terms they don't really understand ... just tell me what it is you need to tell me!"

KEVIN, PART-TIME TUTOR
"Students struggle with addressing the question sometimes, because, whether it's in coursework or in exams, they want to tell you what they know. If they feel confident with the bit that they know about, so as long as it has some vague relationship to what you've asked, then they're going to tell you all about it."

Yasmin, a senior tutor, describes what she means by addressing the question and how tutors are not fooled by waffle. Finally, Kevin, a part-time tutor, has a good insight into why so many students fall into this trap of wanting to write all they know about a topic.

Addressing (Answering) the Question
Action Points

→ Find an essay you have written in the past – it doesn't have to be one you have done at university – and mark it as if you were the tutor, looking particularly at how much of it directly answers the question and how much of it is writing everything you know about the topic.

→ If it's 100% answering the question, well done! If it's less than that, then think how you would rewrite those irrelevant parts to make them answer the question. In some cases whole paragraphs might have to be scrapped altogether as they just do not fit. This is a hard and painful lesson for all who write, not just students.

→ Have a look at some essay titles and see if you can break them down into the topic area and the actual instruction (ie. what you have to do).

→ Be a ruthless 'waffle detective' – see if friends will allow you to look at their essays and spot the waffle, and ask them to do the same for you.

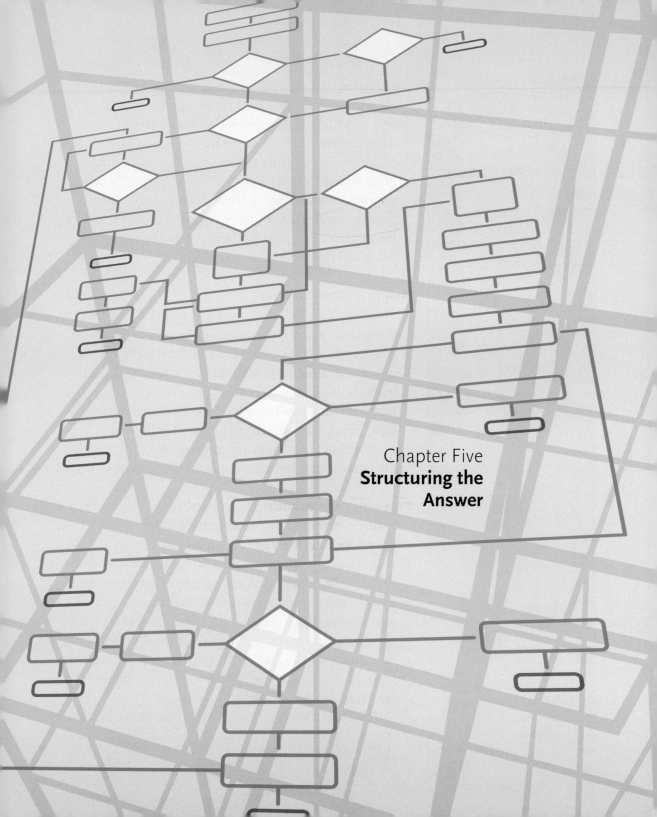

Chapter Five
**Structuring the
Answer**

Chapter Five
Structuring the Answer

Introduction

How to structure an essay may seem on the surface a very easy thing to do; however, this is an area of essay writing where students frequently do not do so well. The problem of structuring an answer is that many students jump straight into their answer without properly planning what they are going say and in what order they are going to say it. This chapter will look at how to structure the essay answer, some of the more common mistakes made and how to avoid them.

How to structure an essay

Since writing a well-structured essay can be a difficult thing to do, where do you begin? Typically, most advice will tell you to think of the essay in three parts: the introduction, the main body and the conclusion. All three parts are absolutely essential to any piece of writing, but it is surprising how many students go straight into a topic without introducing it, or tail off at the end of an essay without coming to any conclusion. Let us start with the introduction and see what the students have to say:

Start with the introduction

Both Helen and Zhang explain that the introduction tells the reader what is going to be in the essay. They also make the same point: that the basic structure is embedded in the introduction. This is a good strategy to employ, as it alerts the readers to the overall structure of your essay and prepares them for the ideas you will explore in more detail in the rest of the work. If you then follow the structure you've laid out in the introduction by considering each main point one-by-one throughout the rest of the essay, your essay will be well-structured.

This leads us on to the next part of the structure: the

main body. This is the part of the essay which presents your answer to the question: it will contain all the arguments that you want to discuss and all the theoretical concepts that you want to evaluate. Ajay, a second-year student, raises another important aspect of structuring an essay, which is about its 'flow'.

If you want to avoid your essay reading like a shopping list which consists of unrelated pieces of information, you need to make links between one point and the next, always keeping in mind how the points relate back to the essay title, as Chloe explains.

Her comment explains that the structure of your answer is dependent on addressing the question, and therefore, as mentioned in Chapter Four, you have to break the question down into small parts and then tackle each part, which will then give you a platform from which you can structure your essay.

The final part of any piece of writing should be the conclusion. A general piece of advice is to make sure your last paragraph directly refers back to the essay title itself. The conclusion is not a place for introducing any new material or ideas, but should be a direct response to the essay question in the title. It is the logical culmination of what you have been writing about in the main body of the essay and should provide a satisfying end point.

Planning your answer

In order to have a well-structured essay, you need to plan what you are going to say in advance of writing the essay. Some students find it helpful to write down all the points that they want to make and then work out how these points relate to one another, as well as the order in which they want to present them in the main body of the essay.

HELEN, 3RD-YEAR STUDENT, EXPLAINS WHAT SHE DOES
"I always have an introduction which tells the tutor how I am going to structure the essay, and then I will make my points in an order which answers the question best."

ZHANG'S SIMILAR APPROACH
"In your introduction you say what you're going to be looking at and your basic structure and then follow it from there."

AJAY, 2ND-YEAR STUDENT
"You must always have a few points to make, and then you make them and relate them to each other, and then you have an answer which is structured and puts your point across."

CHLOE EXPLAINS HOW SHE STRUCTURES ESSAYS
"Introduction and major focus, main body and conclusion, and making sure you're actually answering the question and stick to that, really. The rest of the answer just relies on the question."

Hannah tells us
how she does it
"You probably start off with some prior research into the area, and then move on to more recent research, different theories and perspectives, and then structure your answer to fit all these in some sort of methodical way. Then do a conclusion at the end which ties everything together."

Sam, 3rd-year student
"If you've got your essay in sections and you are talking about a person's age, keep age together. Don't talk about age in one section, then talk about something else and then go back to age. Similar information is kept together and then flows on to something else so it all makes sense."

Chen emphasises flow
"Have a clear beginning, middle and end. Make sure that when you write about something or someone, don't keep going back to it in different paragraphs, otherwise it doesn't flow and you don't have a good, structured essay."

As you can see from what Hannah says, she, like the other more experienced essay writers, is keenly aware of the fundamental importance of building a structure which answers the question.

Essay flow

We mentioned the word 'flow' a little earlier when we referred to the need to avoid a shopping-list type of essay. Flow is important because it enables your tutor to read your answer easily and know immediately what your viewpoint or argument is. Sam, a third-year student, explains his understanding of flow.

His point is a good one to remember. If you write about something and then four paragraphs later write about it again, your essay is not very well-structured, as the reader has to go back to the original paragraph to remember what you've already written. Our advice is that if you write about something in one paragraph then don't revisit it later in the essay, as you will probably be repeating yourself. When you repeat points, your essay does not flow and ultimately you may be penalized for poor structure. Chen emphasises this point from his own experience.

Tutors' views on structuring the answer

Many of the tutors that we spoke to seemed to have strong opinions about what makes a well-structured essay and what doesn't. The overwhelming opinion was that it needs a clear introduction and then a section dealing with the issues and problems, then a conclusion. It needs to be well-structured – not all over the place. Take time to put arguments together carefully.

This may seem a very basic explanation; however, the structure of an essay doesn't need to be complicated. The key thing to remember is that you must make your essay easy to read and your arguments easy to follow. Daniel, a senior tutor, explains what he means by structuring the answer.

What he says here is well worth having a good think about, as it really gets into the actual logistics of an essay, both at the level of the overall essay itself and at the level of each constituent paragraph. Structuring is a skill and one that, like all the essay writing skills, gets better with practice. To help yourself improve, try remembering the simple maxim of one idea for each paragraph. This will help with the structure and also make it easier for the reader to follow your arguments throughout the essay.

Carefully thought out and coherent writing is important when you want to achieve the best possible mark with regard to structuring your answer. Your tutor needs to know your perspective or response to the essay question, and a good structure will enable all the arguments to flow together to make your response clear. [Tutor's comments continued overleaf →]

DANIEL, SENIOR TUTOR

"Structure is at a macro and a micro level. An essay needs an introduction and a conclusion, but also paragraphs that link together, so an argument is structured and therefore fluid. And appropriate structure within each paragraph; so, one idea – one paragraph. Sentences where they should be, those kinds of things. That kind of micro level structure I would also comment on if it was particularly inappropriate, and I have seen people write one-sentence paragraphs – bad idea – and one-page paragraphs, which every now and again might be appropriate, but that would be a huge idea and there's probably a way to split that down and make that easier to read."

SHARON, TUTOR

"Always keep the question in mind and think about what story you're telling – make it logical and linear. If you go along a certain route make the conclusion logical to that route. It should work as a coherent essay, rather than 'I know I need to throw in something about this and I need to include that'. And sometimes that happens half-way through – you're reading an essay and it's all going terribly well, and it's like the student suddenly thought 'oh no, I haven't mentioned...', and they just put things in."

Sharon, a tutor, has this advice about making it easier for the reader to follow your arguments throughout your essays.

Structuring the Answer
Action Points

→ Find a piece of your writing and look at it to see if you have followed the 'one idea per paragraph rule'.

→ Try re-organising any paragraphs that have more than one idea into smaller paragraphs, and see if that improves the clarity of your writing.

→ Some examples of useful linking phrases that will help the flow of your essay are:
"Having explored xxx, the next issue to consider is xxx ..."
"Turning to the other side of the argument ..."
"So far, xxx has been considered, but the evidence has not yet been examined. In this next section, research studies from xxx will be evaluated ..."

→ List some linking phrases that you have noticed in other people's writing and build up your own collection.

understanding

Chapter Six
Demonstrating Understanding

Introduction

One of the things that students sometimes don't realise about essay writing is that tutors are looking for a demonstration that they have understood the theory, concept or research they are writing about. This is why the (misguided) belief that it is important to tell tutors everything they know about a subject is so common when students first start writing essays. This way of writing is also extremely prevalent in examination essays. In this chapter, we look at some of the difficulties students face when trying to develop their own understanding of a topic and at ways of best demonstrating their understanding in written work.

Read, read, read... and then read some more!

The majority of the students we talked to quite correctly linked developing understanding with doing research for their essays. In order to write a good essay, it is vital to read books and journals to develop your understanding of the topic area. Research is a major activity at university, and if you can start to practise it in the first year, it sets you up for a far easier time in the later years when research becomes crucial for getting higher marks.

Experienced students might develop their understanding by beginning with a search around the area; this could be through consulting a book or some journals or the internet (although you have to be very careful indeed when using the internet for your research – see Chapter Nine). This helps students get a clearer idea of what the topic is about, which is the first step in developing understanding.

Increasing your general knowledge is also important, and is something that develops throughout your life. If you become well read in your first year, then your general knowledge will increase and this will help you to understand topics at a deeper level as you progress through your degree.

Lana offers some excellent advice to those students who struggle to understand what tutors have told them in the lectures. What she is saying here is that it is often very difficult to understand new concepts in a lecture, and what you have to do is read up on them afterwards. What she also says about how hard this can be is a very important truth. Learning something new does not come easily. Often you have to read more than one source to help you understand something, and often you have to read texts over and over again before they start to make any sense. Many first-year students tend just to take down notes in lectures and then forget about them. This is not a very useful habit to get into. If, however, you start in the first year to re-read your notes and read more on topics that you didn't understand very well in the lectures, then your understanding will develop. It is hard work, but it is worth it, not only because it will help you in both coursework and examination essays, but also because it is a real thrill to wrestle with a difficult concept and eventually crack it.

Phil, a third-year student, knows how important it is to show how well you understand the larger context of what you are writing about. Kyoko, another third-year student, has also learned how important reading and researching a topic is.

As mentioned in previous chapters, the first year is an introduction to the way you will be assessed at university. It should be a comfort to realise that you are not expected to start your degree understanding everything. Our advice is to begin thinking about how you are going to develop your understanding as early as possible,

LANA OFFERS THIS ADVICE
"In your lecture notes, if you don't understand something you try and find a book or a study that might help you understand it better. Sometimes articles are so hard to understand. It is very difficult. You need to find as many articles as you can in order to gain understanding."

PHIL, 3RD-YEAR STUDENT
"Show the tutor that you have understood not only the essay question but also the whole module, including all the lectures that you've been to."

KYOKO, 3RD-YEAR STUDENT
"I have learned to research a lot more. In the first year it's more spoonfed to you — where to go, what books to read. Now it's more up to you to go and find the resources... you are a lot more independent."

as this will help you adapt quickly to the demands of Higher Education as well as stand you in good stead in future years. Always in degree studies, the emphasis is on developing your abilities, understanding and skills, so that by the time you reach your final year, the expectation will be for you to do much more independent research. (This doesn't mean knowing everything – not even tutors can claim that! In fact, it is sometimes said that the more expert or knowledgeable you are about a subject, the more you realise how much there is still left to discover.)

Look at both sides of the argument

Many of the students we spoke to said they used to read the literature and then just write about it in their essays. However, some students talked about weighing up both sides of an argument. This is a much better strategy, as it means you are able to understand the perspectives and reasoning on both sides of an issue. Reading in such a way that allows you to achieve this kind of understanding will also help you to form opinions about which perspectives and arguments you find most convincing and which ones you disagree with. Lana tells us her idea of what it means to develop understanding.

Beth, a second-year student, has a similar approach, but stresses her own part in the process. This is an excellent example of how an independent learner goes about the task of understanding and weighing up the merit of different arguments.

The concept of justifying your position in relation to the different, sometimes opposing, arguments you have read can be quite difficult at first, but by doing what Lana and Beth do, you will find it gets progressively easier.

LANA ON UNDERSTANDING
"It's about the whole term of development – arguing things in different ways and looking at them from many angles, not necessarily just understanding something from one person's viewpoint, but looking at it in lots of different ways."

BETH, 2ND-YEAR STUDENT
"I develop my understanding by looking at the arguments put across and then making up my own mind who I agree with."

Understand what you are writing about

As mentioned earlier in this book, a common problem in many essay answers is that students tend to write down all they can find on a topic and then expect to do well. This strategy has a major drawback in terms of demonstrating your understanding. When Sanjeev, a second-year student, was asked what he thought demonstrating understanding in an essay was about, he explained why you shouldn't just write down what you find.

His point is important to remember. Tutors are very familiar with the arguments and writings in their respective fields of expertise, and they therefore find it easy to identify information that has come from certain sources (such as textbooks and key journal articles). Their familiarity with these writings also means that they are very good at spotting phrasing which is similar to that in the original source. When you read around a particular topic, your job, therefore, is to decide which arguments are relevant to your particular essay answer (and why you think so), and then to write about these arguments in your own words. Demonstrating your understanding is not the same thing as writing all you know about a topic in an effort to show the tutor you can read a number of books and journals. The process of developing your understanding involves analysing large amounts of information and coming to some sort of personal understanding of a subject that you did not have before you started reading and thinking in depth about it. This is what real learning is about, and demonstrating this understanding is one of the hallmarks of a good essay. Janet tells us why this is important.

SANJEEV, 2ND-YEAR STUDENT
"It is showing the marker that you have understood the topic and the question itself and that you haven't just simply written stuff down from a book. If you do that you haven't really understood what is required."

JANET ON DEMONSTRATING UNDERSTANDING
"It's hard because sometimes you can have so much information at your fingertips and you have to decide what you understand, as you shouldn't put stuff into an essay that you yourself don't understand, otherwise you might have it totally wrong."

Tutors' views on demonstrating understanding

COLIN, SENIOR TUTOR

"I am looking for evidence that students have understood the theory, concept or research they are writing about. Many just give me a mere description, and even if this is accurate, it still doesn't provide me with evidence of understanding."

ANITA, TUTOR

"Letting your reader know that you know why you have included something in your essay will help demonstrate your understanding of what you are writing about."

ALAN, TUTOR, OFFERS HIS OPINION ON PLAGIARISM

"A lot of students think they can get away with plagiarism. Using your own words does not mean rearranging the sentence you have read."

The general opinion of tutors echoes the main principles shown in the students' comments. Many, such as Colin, a senior tutor, want to see evidence of understanding. This supports what the students were saying in their responses. The key is to genuinely set out to understand what you are reading, and when you do this, it will clearly show in the essay answer. Anita is a tutor who has a good piece of advice.

This is closely linked with the criteria of addressing the question, structuring your answer and developing an argument, all of which contribute to your being able to demonstrate your own understanding in an essay. Remember, explaining something so someone else can understand it usually tells the reader that you do, indeed, understand what you are writing about.

Apart from the necessity of demonstrating understanding, there is another important reason why you should struggle to express ideas in your own words, which is to avoid the danger of plagiarism. The tutors we spoke to had some strong views about students simply copying down what they had read in books or changing sentences slightly so as to make it look as if they had written the words themselves.

Plagiarism is a very serious offence at all universities, and every university has a clearly stated policy on what it means and the penalties for committing it. If you try to pass off other people's views or work as your own, this is plagiarism, and it could mean your work will be failed. In order to avoid this, you need to read the literature and try to include the points you want to make in your essay using your own words. This will also allow you to demonstrate that you have understood what you have read in the literature.

Chapter Six
Demonstrating Understanding
Action Points

→ Do you know where your university's plagiarism policy is stated? If not, find it and read it carefully.

→ If there is anything in the plagiarism policy that you don't understand, find out about it before you write your next essay.

→ To brush up your knowledge, have a go at Ted Frick's fun, helpful and very informative quiz on plagiarism available at this website:
http://www.indiana.edu/~tedfrick/plagiarism/

Chapter Seven
Developing Argument

Chapter Seven
Developing Argument

Introduction

An argument is something we have all experienced in our ordinary, day-to-day lives. Sometimes an argument can get heated and impulsive and result in mutual hurling of offensive remarks at the other person – or worse. Argument in an academic sense means something rather different; instead of being aggressive and emotional, it is calm and logical, and it uses evidence rather than unsupported opinion to make a point. An academic argument is sometimes called a thesis, which involves taking a stance on a topic and then proceeding to build a case to persuade the reader that your stance is convincing and justified. In doing this, you have to consider counter-arguments and then explain why they are not as credible as your argument. Sometimes students believe that if they put forward an argument that the tutor does not personally agree with, they will be marked down. This is not the case. When tutors are marking your work, they are looking at the way you have gone about building up a case, and it is the quality of this aspect of your argument that will determine the mark a tutor gives.

An argument can also be defined as a logical arrangement and presentation of ideas which builds towards a justified conclusion. Academic argument is at the very heart of university study, and it is closely linked to what we mean when we talk about critical thinking. During the course of your degree, you will learn how to develop an argument not only within the confines of a written essay but also in a more general cognitive and practical sense. This chapter is aimed at identifying how to write a balanced argument that looks at a particular question from more than one perspective, weighs up the relevant evidence, and concludes with a justified commitment to one view or the other.

Appreciate both sides of the argument

When you develop your own argument in an essay, it is essential that you acknowledge and understand both sides of the relevant arguments you read about in the literature. Seeing both sides of other people's arguments is a crucial aspect of demonstrating your own understanding of the issues and building up your own argument in your essay. Jill offered her understanding of what developing an argument means and why looking at different perspectives is so important.

Her insight and experience is very clear here and shows how she has realised that not everything in print is free from bias or error. A published study presents one person's findings and argument in relation to whatever topic is being addressed. Other people will have come up with different findings and different arguments, sometimes in direct opposition to other studies, on the same topic. In order to decide what you think about a topic and which views you find most convincing, you will need to read more than one person's view on every topic you study in the course of your degree, and be prepared to scrutinise these views for possible biases or inaccuracies or faulty reasoning. This kind of close, critical reading and analysis of other people's work is also called 'critical evaluation'; it will be more fully explored in Chapter Nine.

Use of previous research

The concept of reading many different books and journals may seem a little strange or daunting to the new undergraduate; however, if you can manage to develop this skill quickly in your first year it will make it far easier to develop well-structured and sound arguments in your written work. Julia explains her understanding of developing an argument and the role research plays overleaf.

RICH EXPLAINS

"You have to look at both sides of the coin; otherwise you're not going to get that absolutely close to it."

JILL COMMENTS

"You have to show that you appreciate there are two sides to every argument. As you progress through the years you tend to realise that just because it is written in a book or a journal article doesn't mean that it is right, because it is just one side of an argument and you need to go and find the other side. You need to look at many different perspectives, challenging ones etc."

JULIA'S UNDERSTANDING
OF DEVELOPING ARGUMENT
"Making sure your essay or piece of work is critical and that you are looking at different arguments, you're not just putting one person's point across. You've looked at different types of research to support it, or when someone has gone against it to prove it wrong, so you have two sides. An argument is becoming critical."

JILL OFFERS THIS ADVICE
"You can't just write something and then say that this is the only view – you have to find other people's arguments that go against what someone has said. You can't just write your own opinions. In my first year I used to write 'I think' all the time and I wondered why I didn't get great marks, and I found out it was because I shouldn't have written this as the tutor was not interested in my opinions but rather in what the research had found."

The essence of the argument according to Julia is to become critical. This is a very important part of your development at university, and it's one of the hardest skills to acquire, particularly in the first year when you may feel you know very little while tutors and authors know everything. Not only is this not true, but many of you may have come from an educational background where you were given information and not encouraged to question or challenge it in any way. In your essays at university, however, your tutors expect you to develop a critical eye by looking at many sources and appreciating that there is more than one viewpoint and that some views are 'better' (that is, more convincing) than others.

Jill touches on an area that many students find confusing – that of being original or putting your own opinions into an essay. While it is true that tutors do want to see your considered views on a topic, it is the way you present these views that is crucial. Assertions of personal opinion tend to be frowned upon in many disciplines, because they are unsupported by evidence gathered from your reading. A personal stance or commitment on an issue, arrived at after weighing up all the pros and cons of different perspectives, is what tutors are looking for. This is very different from mere personal opinion. It is still a personal and original response, but it is also measured, balanced and objective and is based on evidence rather than on personal beliefs or feelings. Kyoko shows how she tackles the need to be critical by using research to back up her views [facing page].

Her point about 'telling the reader a story' is also important to remember. The best way to write an essay is to write for your tutor, who you know is knowledgeable on the topic you are writing about, but who is looking for a demonstration that you can put the relevant arguments forward and critically analyse them. Sean makes a very good point below about learning how to develop an argument by reading journal articles.

He has found out that in some journals the arguments tend to go across many articles and sometimes issues. Reading an exchange in a journal is a really good way of learning how to critically analyse a piece of research. Many of the articles will comment upon previous articles, and reading through these articles help you to learn more about the typical style used by authors writing in the field. [Continued overleaf →]

KYOKO ON BEING CRITICAL
"I want to make sure I am explaining what I'm talking about and actually developing an argument. By this I mean that I am critically analysing something from a different perspective to my own. So it's looking at, say, two opposing arguments and trying to tell the reader what these arguments are, how they differ and who else has contributed to the arguments within the research area. It's like telling a story and using previous research to back it up."

SEAN MAKES THIS POINT
"It's the same as what happens in lots of the journals I have read. They always have one person saying one thing, then someone else attacks them saying another. I have seen it go on for many papers. Since seeing this I have now started to do this in my essays. I look at both sides of the argument and write about what each side says, and then offer a critical opinion of my own without making sweeping statements I can't back up."

SANJEEV ON BALANCE

"In my arguments I always think it's important to show both sides – like the positive and negative aspects. If you don't do so, then you are showing a certain amount of bias."

JANET ON STRUCTURE

"Developing an argument also ties in very strongly with structuring the answer in terms of clarity of thoughts."

LANA AGREES

"Developing an argument means you don't just have lots of separate paragraphs, they're all building up the discussion, which is about structuring the answer. I don't know how you would do one without the other really."

BETH ON FLOWING ARGUMENT

"You have an argument, which is the basis of your essay, and you've got to have a flow which goes from beginning to end. Sometimes it's easy to just copy information from a book and cite essays and stuff without really having a flow explaining why you said it."

Avoiding bias

We have looked at the benefits of looking at both sides of the argument: it is important that however strongly you might feel that there is only one answer, you nevertheless provide a balanced essay. Sanjeev understands this.

Links to other assessment criteria

In previous chapters we looked in detail at some of the other core assessment criteria; however, as already pointed out, each assessment criterion relates to all of the others. When Janet was asked about developing an argument, she realised that in order to do so you need to have a good structure so that you can show your clear, logical thinking. Lana also emphasises this point.

Making your argument flow

In our last chapter we mentioned the importance of making your essay flow. Linked to this is the concept of flow within your argument, as Beth identifies below.

Other students also had a viewpoint on flow in an argument. Some start with a definition to introduce the marker to the topic. From there they might go into the actual development of the argument by referring to data and theories, and then evaluate them, coming back to critical evaluation.

Chapter Seven
Developing
Argument
Action Points

→ Take the following contentious statement and think through your position on it:
"Higher education should be available to anyone who wants it, regardless of academic ability."

→ Jot down the main points in your argument and then note as many counter-arguments as you can think of and how you would deal with each in an objective and balanced way.

Chapter Eight
Use of Evidence

Chapter Eight
Use of Evidence

Introduction

This assessment criterion can be confusing and sometimes causes problems for students, particularly when they are writing their first essay at undergraduate level. The confusion comes from not fully understanding what is meant by voicing your own opinion in the context of an academic essay. At university, you are required to write about what others have found and argued, and yet, at the same time, your tutors will tell you that they want you to think for yourselves and come up with your own ideas and interpretations. So how can you resolve these two, contradictory requirements? It wouldn't be fair of us to pretend that this fine balance is easy, but accomplishing it definitely does get better with practice. What skilled essay writers do is put forward a response to the essay question that is uniquely theirs by:

- reading the relevant sources
- formulating an argument that represents their personal stance
- ensuring that all the points they make in their essays are supported with evidence from the literature.

Supporting your points

In our day-to-day lives, when we tell others about something new or talk about a topic they are not familiar with, we can just tell them our thoughts and they tend to take what we say at face value (sometimes, but not always!). In essay writing, you cannot make claims about knowledge without backing them up with reference to the appropriate sources. Lana talks about this in detail. Jill also comments upon this, but she looked at it from what she thought the tutors wanted. Ranjit also comments upon this [facing page].

Jill's and Ranjit's comments emphasise the need for you to search through relevant journals and find previous research in order to support your points. You have to show the tutor that you have done this by referencing these sources throughout your essay.

Getting good information

As with any form of investigation, you will gather lots of information and resources but some of them will not be relevant to the particular area that you are studying. The skill in gathering information is to be able to distinguish what is relevant to your particular essay and what is not. Janet explains what she understands by this, and Lana also comments on this subject.

Her point is crucial to your use of evidence. Using many different good sources of information will demonstrate to your tutor that you have a solid understanding of the relevant issues and the argument you are putting forward. These sources could be journals, some textbooks and other credible documents. Using these sources will give you the opportunity to demonstrate a balanced view of the area you are writing about.

The perils of using quotes

Depending on the subject you study, the use of quotes in an essay may or may not be approved of. In English Literature essays, for example, it would be hard to imagine how you could write a critique of a text without extensive quotes. In Psychology, however, the position is very different and the general rule of thumb is to avoid them wherever possible. This is for two main reasons. The first is that your own understanding of something really only emerges once you try to explain it to someone else by putting it into your own words. The second

LANA BACKS UP HER CLAIMS
"You get an article or a book that proves your point. It's not off the top of my head, someone else has found this."

JILL ON TUTORS' WANTS
"They want everything backed up by previous research. You can't just make a point and leave it at that, you need to show the evidence is out there. This has been said and it is in this journal or this book."

RANJIT SUPPORTS HIS POINTS
"It must be scientific. You can't just say, 'well, um, generally speaking, this causes that' – you must give proof for that."

JANET EXPLAINS RELEVANCE
"Use relevant information from the literature that helps you to give a balanced argument. Get good journals and use them to help you answer the question correctly."

LANA COMMENTS
"A wide range of examples shows that you have some understanding of the different schools of thought."

reason is that although an essay full of quotes with a few connecting sentences is not technically plagiarism (presuming you have followed the correct conventions), it is, at best, a very superficial response to the question, as you haven't demonstrated your own understanding of what other people have said.

Rich, a second-year student, is learning that using quotes is not a good idea. His comment is interesting not only for what he has to say about quotes, but also for what he has to say about acting on tutor feedback. This is the best way of improving your essay writing, yet we often heard from students that they only bother with the mark and don't take any notice of the feedback. It's hard to imagine how any human being could improve on any skill or ability, be it gymnastics, opera singing or driving a car, without taking careful notice of their trainer's advice and feedback. Exactly the same principle applies to essay writing: careful attention to feedback and application of what has been learned in future work will greatly facilitate the improvement of your essay writing skills.

The importance of using journals

When we talked to students, many of them described how they initially went about using evidence and how they have noticed a considerable amount of progress since then. Lauren, a third-year student, describes how it happened to her.

Lauren's experience is very similar to that of many students, which is why in previous chapters we have talked about the benefits of getting to grips with using more resources right from the start of your university life. The benefits of using journal articles are huge: the quality and quantity of your evidence will increase greatly and so will your understanding of the topic area.

RICH ON USING QUOTES

"It is sometimes difficult to choose exactly which quote to include, how to make it relevant, and show why you've chosen that particular quote. I know this from feedback I've had on my essays – 'don't use so many quotes and establish why you use them', basically. 'What was the point? Why was what that person said better than something else?' "

LAUREN'S PROGRESS
WITH VARIOUS RESOURCES

"When I was a first- or second-year student, I don't remember using any journals, but in the third year I used them more. I guess it's about using different kinds of resources. I still use books but I'm not as dependent on them as I was earlier."

Journal articles are how researchers report their findings and challenge the findings of others in the topic area; they are almost like topic-based newspapers (without the comic strips and star signs pages!) where researchers engage in a continuous conversation, or academic dialogue, with each other. Reading relevant journals makes achieving the assessment criterion of use of evidence a lot easier for you. Articles provide you with many arguments for and against theories and other researchers' work. Again, the skill – and this is something you will become much better at over time – is to be able to identify what is relevant and what is not.

Sean now realises that he should have used lots of journals to provide evidence to back up the points he made. He also realises that the problem was that he didn't do this right from the start of his degree.

Referencing your sources accurately

Using evidence in essays has to be done correctly and this means accurate referencing. This is essential in Higher Education. If you write about what someone has researched, then you must show where you got the information, both:

- in the text, by putting in brackets the author's surname and the date when the study was published;
- and in the reference section at the end of your essay, by alphabetically listing, by author, all journals, books, websites and other sources you referred to in the main text of your essay.

SEAN ON USING JOURNALS
"When I research a topic I try to find lots of journals about the topic so that I can get a balanced view of the area, and then I try and incorporate as many references to present literature and research as I can. At the start of my degree I didn't do that and I think that is one of the reasons that I didn't do very well."

....

MAGDA, SENIOR TUTOR

"With first-years in particular, they never, ever include the references. All the studies they talk about they don't reference. So I knock a few marks off for that because I want to make a point. I mean, they are told how to do it but they don't bother. And sometimes they don't seem to understand what they're talking about, so it's important to see that they know what they're writing about."

....

ROGER, PART-TIME TUTOR

"I don't think they get what they're asked to do. They don't really listen to you. Actually, it's written down in this very lengthy document. I think they think they've got to show they've read stuff and so they paraphrase and plagiarise."

Magda, a senior tutor, explains her experiences of first-year essays in relation to referencing. She talks about the lack of referencing and how that directly affects how she marks the essays. This is an important point for all students, whether they are in their first, second or final year of study. Magda also says that all the first-years are told that they have to reference everything that they use in their assignments. She, along with many other tutors, takes the view that when students have been told how to do something in their writing and then do not do it, it is valid to penalise them by lowering the mark.

Carrying on with this theme, Roger, a part-time tutor, has a somewhat negative view of first-year students in relation to understanding what they are told about referencing. His comment should sound alarm bells to all students. This guide is definitely not telling you to copy large chunks from textbooks and journals to prove to the tutor that you have read around the subject, because if you do you will be plagiarising. Our advice here is that if you read something in a book or a journal and you want to write about it in your essay, you must write about it in your own words and always remember to reference it in the text as well as include it in the reference section at the end of the essay. By doing this, you are showing the tutor that you have read around the subject, and you are also demonstrating that you have understood what you have read and that you can apply this understanding to the question you are attempting to answer.

Use of Evidence
Action Points

→ Referencing is quite simple if you remember this 'rule': **Every single name that appears in anything you write must be followed by a date in brackets, and the full reference must be presented at the end of your assignment.**

→ Write this rule down and display it prominently so that you don't forget it.

→ Try the 'Spot the Referencing Mistakes' quiz on the next page.

The following excerpt has been adapted from an article by Norton (2004) to incorporate some common mistakes. Can you spot them all? *See page 121 for the answers.*

Norton, L.S. (2004). Using assessment criteria as learning criteria. A case study using Psychology Applied Learning Scenarios (PALS). *Assessment & Evaluation in Higher Education*, 29(6), 687-702.

According to Hornby, assessment has four main roles: formative, to provide support for future learning; summative, to provide information about performance at the end of a course; certification, selecting by means of qualification; evaluative, a means by which stakeholders can judge the effectiveness of the system as a whole. Such a list is fairly typical but it omits one of the most powerful roles that assessment can have, its effect not only on what students learn but how they learn. Graham Gibbs (1999) has suggested that since students see assessment as the curriculum, effective teaching needs to use this knowledge in order to use the power of assessment strategically to help students learn. Biggs (2002) makes the same point when he says that students learn what they think will be assessed rather than what is in the curriculum. This means that one of the pedagogical benefits of assessment is that it can be used to act as a lever to make students actively engage with a given task. Examinations have traditionally been used for this purpose throughout the entire history of Higher Education, but the nature of the learning that they engender is frequently passive and non-transformative (Scouller, 1998, *Higher Education*, 28 (4) 435-454).

References

Biggs, J. (2003). Aligning teaching and assessing to course objectives, paper presented at the International Conference on Teaching and Learning in Higher Education: New trends and Innovations, University of Averio, 13-17 April 2003. Available online at: http://event.ua.pt/iched/.

Hornby, W. (2003). Assessing using grade-related criteria: a single currency for universities? *Assessment & Evaluation in Higher Education*, 28(4), 435-454.

Scouller, K. M. (1998). The influence of assessment method on students' learning approaches: multiple choice question examination versus assignment essay.

Chapter Nine
Evaluation

Chapter Nine
Evaluation

Introduction

Evaluation is the criterion which tends to separate the 'excellent' from the 'good' or the 'competent' essay. As well as referring to primary sources such as journal papers reporting on empirical research, tutors are looking for evidence that you have evaluated that research. For example, you may have to ask yourself such questions as: 'Is it a convincing research study?' or 'Is it methodologically sound?' or 'Do the authors claim too much from their findings?' The important thing to remember is that you should always be questioning what you are reading and not taking things at face value. This chapter will show you what the students we asked understood by evaluation and how you can improve on your evaluation skills. As always, we include some tutors' comments so you know what they are looking for.

Strengths and weaknesses

The majority of the students we spoke to said they understood evaluation to be: 'strengths and weaknesses of a certain approach or an idea'. By this many of them thought that in order to evaluate something you have to demonstrate both the strengths and weakness of it. This could be related to a theory or indeed a research study. The skill is to be able to explain to the reader why you think it is a strength or a weakness. Jill explains this on the facing page.

Learning to read with a critical eye is not easy. It takes lots of practice but the more you read, the easier it will become. The benefits of doing this are that when it comes to your own writing you will be able to cite arguments and evidence from your reading, but also acknowledge that such sources should not always be taken 'at face value'. If you concentrate on weighing up the strengths and the weaknesses of your sources, you will demonstrate a far greater understanding of the topic and will show your tutor that you can evaluate your reading. In fact, Lana goes even further with this point, showing a sophisticated understanding of what it means to critically evaluate.

Different viewpoints

It is very important that your evaluation takes into account differing viewpoints on the same subject. As mentioned in the section on strengths and weakness above, it is possible for all topics and ideas to be looked at from different angles.

The important thing to remember is that you have to weigh up both sides of an argument and convince the reader that your conclusions are based on a sound and logical reasoning process. Ranjit explained what he does when he is trying to evaluate something and Janet also summarises this point concisely.

Being critical

As you progress through university, being critical will become easier for you to do. The idea is that you read something and the first thing you think about in response is: 'Do I agree with that, and if so, why?', 'If I don't agree with it, why not?', 'Can I evaluate this critically?'. Rich explains what the indicators of being critical are.

He hits on a fundamental truth in the whole business of Higher Education, which is about developing your own position on what you are told or what you read rather than accepting it unquestioningly. Generally, what you are taught in your lectures is there to encourage you to go away and investigate further so that you can

JILL EXPLAINS

"Look at the strengths and weaknesses of what you read. Can you think of any alternative explanations for the claims that the theory or research makes? If so, bring them into your essay, and if possible support them with evidence."

LANA ON EVALUATION

"I think it is more than strengths and weaknesses. It's actually criticising their strengths and weaknesses."

RANJIT'S APPROACH

"Take two opposing theories, discuss them and see what the evidence is for one and the counter-evidence for the other."

JANET SUMMARISES

"A clear outline of what you've looked at, from various angles."

RICH EXPLAINS BEING CRITICAL

"Not taking something as said. Looking at it and thinking 'Is that true?', 'Are there any weaknesses or strengths, or can it be improved?' Just being more critical about whatever it is that you're reading."

LAUREN ON BEING CRITICAL

"Just because something's been taught in a lecture doesn't mean it's right, so it's about looking at it and saying whether you think you agree with it, rather than just writing it down. We are taught this model – well, what do I think of it?"

"You need some differing opinions as well, those who criticise, and those who say, 'no, it's good'. Bumping opinions against each other."

A TUTOR ON STUDENTS' AWARENESS OF EVALUATION

"They don't know what evaluation is, especially in the first year."

YASMIN, SENIOR TUTOR

"Evaluating is one of the things that I personally pay more attention to if I'm trying to decide if an essay is merely acceptable or good."

formulate your own opinions and views on the information. In a sense then, you can evaluate whether what you have been told is what you agree with, and this skill can be translated into your essay writing. Lauren's comments relate specifically to what she was told in her lectures.

Tutors' views on evaluation

As elsewhere in this book, we look at what tutors have said about certain assessment criteria. According to tutors, evaluation is very important as it demonstrates a high level of understanding and application, essential for the higher grades.

Students tend to be unaware of evaluation

We asked tutors what they thought generally about whether students were aware of evaluation. Many of them commented negatively. This is not a major problem for students at the beginning of their degree study, as tutors don't expect an advanced level of evaluation in the first year. However, if you can start to be more evaluative in your work right from an early stage, then you will be in a very strong position in future years.

How to get higher marks

As we have said before, taking an evaluative approach to your essays is crucial in order to get the very highest marks. Many tutors concentrate specifically on this assessment criterion when deciding which essays should receive higher marks. Yasmin, a senior tutor, comments.

Distinguishing between very good essays and good essays is difficult for tutors. Many will have to mark a lot of essays in a relatively short space of time. Therefore, if you want yours to stand out as one of the very good ones, making sure your essay is evaluative will help you do this.

Being critical

Evaluation is, by its very nature, a process that involves being critical. Ade describes why this is so.

This means going beyond just describing an argument; it means thinking carefully about what you're saying, thinking through the issues and being critical of what you read, even of what you decide to use as your supportive evidence. The reason why this is considered so important in an essay is because it demonstrates to your tutor that you are aware that there is more than one perspective on the essay topic and that some perspectives have more to offer than others, but that no one perspective offers a complete explanation.

ADE, TUTOR

"Evaluation includes potential for criticism, which entails thinking about theory in relation to both evidence and other theories. For example, does the theory stand up in light of empirical evidence?; does another theory do a better job of explaining the evidence?"

Evaluation
Action Points

→ What do you understand to be the difference between 'evaluation' and 'critical evaluation'?

→ The following questions are adapted from materials provided by Sandra Sinfield, Learning Development Coordinator at London Metropolitan University, and used in the Assessment Plus workshops available on the website: www.writenow.ac.uk/assessmentplus.

Reading questions
When you read your next chapter or article, ask yourself these questions. The answers will help you read and write with a critically evaluative perspective.

1 | What is this paragraph about?

2 | What is the author's angle? How do I know?

3 | What is the argument?

4 | What is the evidence?

5 | Is the evidence valid? How do I know?

6 | Is the evidence relevant? How do I know?

7 | Have I heard / read anything similar or dissimilar? What was it?

8 | Do I agree or disagree? Why?

Chapter Ten
**Writing
Exam Essays**

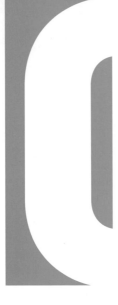

Chapter Ten
Writing
Exam Essays

Introduction

Much of what we have written about in this book applies equally well to essays that you write in examinations, but what you need to remember here is that although the assessment criteria are the same, tutors will interpret them more leniently when marking exam answers. Here we focus on just two of the criteria: addressing the question (the most important thing you can do in an exam) and structuring your answer (the best way of making sure you have addressed the question).

Difficulties in exams

Many students do not like exams due to the pressures and time constraints put upon them. Carol, a second-year student, comments on this on the facing page.

Our advice is not to panic. In an exam situation when tensions are running high, it's easy to feel pressured into writing straight away, particularly if everyone around you is doing just that. This is probably the worst thing you can do. Take a few moments to breathe deeply, try to relax and really read the question paper thoroughly. Make sure you know how many questions you have to answer and that you attempt them all. You will not get higher marks for doing two splendid essays and not attempting the third one because you have run out of time or because you don't know much about the topic. Here's an illustration of the consequences of not answering all three questions that are equally weighted in a three-question paper.

Another important reason for taking some time at the start of an exam is to give yourself the opportunity to think hard about what each question is asking you to do. If you start writing straight away, the chances are you will fall into the old trap mentioned earlier in this book of writing everything you can remember about a subject.

The case of Jane

Jane looks at her exam paper and realises she can answer two questions, but that all the others are really hard and she only knows a little about each of them.

Jane decides the best thing to do is to spend most of her time on the question she knows best and the rest of her time on a second essay, in the hopes that her good marks will pull her through. She doesn't even attempt the third question.

Jane's results

Question One – 70% (excellent A-grade essay) Question Two – 40% (misinterpreted the question slightly and didn't leave herself enough time) Question Three – 0% (wasn't attempted)

The overall mark is the mean of three marks, so Jane gets 36% and fails in spite of her A-grade essay.

The case of Toby

Toby looks at his exam paper and realises he can answer two questions, but that all the others are really hard and he only knows a little about each of them.

Toby knows the importance of making an attempt at three questions so decides to be very strict on portioning out time equally to all three questions, giving himself the best chance of getting at least some marks for his weakest one.

Toby's results

Question One – 55% (a solid average answer) Question Two – 50% (as above, but a bit weaker) Question Three – 25% (he really struggled with this one, but managed to scrape together some marks)

The overall mark is the mean of three marks, so Toby gets 43% and passes in spite of his failed essay.

CAROL, 2ND-YEAR STUDENT, ON THE PRESSURES OF TIME CONSTRAINTS
"Exams are a completely different story. I always worry that I won't have enough time to plan my answer and then I panic and probably don't address the question. The thing is that you are under pressure to write the answers in a short space of time and therefore you have to be quick and I always struggle to plan well for them."

MARK, TUTOR, ON ONE
STUDENT'S FLAWED STRATEGY
*"Addressing the question is
important. One student wrote
a really good essay in the exam
but she didn't answer the
question and her introduction
she said she was ignoring it!
She really shot herself in the
foot because a lot of her cover-
age was relevant to it. In the
end we gave her a C because
there was enough within the
content of the essay and style
for that grade, but really she
could have got an A."*

NATALIE OFFERS THIS ADVICE
*"Have little sub-headings in
your head so you put the right
things in the right places.
It's all about planning, which
is particularly important in
exams when you haven't got a
lot of time. You think 'what do
I want to write?', and I find it
best to plan what I'm going to
put in each section first."*

RUTH PLANS AHEAD
*"Writing a very brief plan of
what you're going to write
before you actually start on
the essay proper."*

Writing everything you can remember about a subject will not get you better marks even in an exam situation. Remember to address the question at all times and not to waffle about the subject.

Addressing the question

As we've mentioned, addressing the question is even more important in an exam situation where time is at an absolute premium and where nerves can make even the best-prepared student feel compelled just to write down everything he or she knows. Mark is a tutor who recalls how not addressing the question had very unfortunate consequences in one of the exam scripts he was marking.

Structuring the answer

Essays that you write in examinations are no different to coursework essays when it comes to structuring an answer. In fact, due to time constraints, it would be far easier and more beneficial for you to plan the essay structure a few minutes before you attempt to write the answer than if you were to leave this initial step out. Natalie, a third-year student, offers this advice.

The problem with exams is that many students do panic and if they haven't planned what they are going to write, they can easily become repetitive and ultimately confused about what they have and have not written about. Many students find it helpful to take a few moments to jot down a small plan before writing their answer, as Ruth does.

Tutor's views on writing exam essays

One useful tip from a senior lecturer in Psychology with a particular interest in assessment was to make sure that you always end your exam answer by directly referring back to the question, even if you run out of time. Make your main points in note form and then write your concluding paragraph in full in which you specifically say how you are answering the question.

Make sure you know what the weighting is

This was mentioned earlier in terms of making sure you divide your time and effort equally if the questions carry equal weight, but quite often they don't, so it is important to know what the weighting is and to act accordingly. Tariq, a postgraduate student, shares his past experience of not taking into account the weighting of each question in an exam.

Finally, it is important to know that tutors appreciate the problems of doing exams and therefore their expectations are not as high for examination answers as they are for coursework essays. The key to being successful at exams is to take control by realising how the assessment weighting for each paper works and keeping a cool head in the exam room.

A SENIOR LECTURER'S TIP
"Remember, exam markers have scores of answers to mark and the last thing they read in your essay is the concluding paragraph – so make it a very strong one. Don't, whatever you do, just tail off or come to a sudden stop."

TARIQ, POSTGRAD STUDENT, ON NOT TAKING WEIGHTING INTO ACCOUNT
"I've done that recently in an exam. Especially when you have two hours and you might have a question that is worth 10% and others worth 5% and you're flying through them and you may spend 15-20 minutes answering a question that is only worth 10% ... later on there's a question worth 50%, and I have cut myself off for time and I have got maybe five or ten minutes to answer it. With exams in particular you have to structure your answers and look through the paper and see what's what. If you have a question worth 5% don't spend ages answering it, because that will mess your overall grade up. "

Writing Exam Essays
Action Points

→ There are many excellent sources of advice on how to do well in exams, and some are listed on pages 124 – 125.

→ One of the best ways of preparing for exams is to practise writing exam answers. It takes a lot of discipline but will pay dividends, as exam writing is a skill that really does get better with practice. The trouble with the university system, though, is that typically you don't get enough practice if you have exams only once a year.

→ Form an exam-writing group with one or two fellow students and set yourselves an hour to write an essay from an old exam paper. Then share what you've written and mark each other's work. If you do this a couple of times, you will be amazed at how much better you get.

Appendix
Students With Special Needs

Introduction

So far in this book we have looked at how students perceive and understand assessment criteria. We have also taken into consideration tutors' opinions and have offered advice about how to use the assessment criteria wisely to produce your essays. For students with special needs, some of this advice might be difficult to follow, depending on the nature of their particular circumstances. In this appendix we report on our interviews with student disability advisors. What emerged from these conversations was that some students have a learning disability but are not aware of it or what steps they could take to overcome it. This chapter will look at each of the criteria in turn and will show how students who do have special learning needs can overcome some of the problems they might face.

Addressing the question

For students with dyslexia, there can be particular problems with understanding the meaning of questions for assignments. The recommendation from disability advisors such as Anne is that they contact their university's Learning Support Centre or equivalent.

Nearly all universities will have some sort of learning support unit where students can go to get help with their essay writing. Often this means making an appointment. What will typically happen is that the advisor will sit down with you and show you how you can break down an essay title, so that you can work out exactly what the tutor wants you to achieve in that assignment.

Another disability advisor, Carmel, reported that she has spoken to a number of students about this assessment criterion of addressing the question.

If you have this learning disability, you are not alone. Carmel also gives an example of a student who came to speak to her and who she thought might be having a problem without knowing it.

Carmel said this is a classic example of a student not being aware of her or his own specific learning difficulty. Luckily for this student, she was able to spot the problem and help him. This does not, of course, mean that if you occasionally find it difficult to understand what an essay title means, you have a specific learning difficulty. Most of us have to wrestle with difficult assignments from time to time! If, however, you always find it practically impossible to understand each assignment that is given to you, and if this has been a regular pattern throughout your education, you might find it helpful to have a chat with your university disability advisor who has a lot of experience and will be able to help you.

If you think that you have a learning disability such as dyslexia, then there is considerable support available, as Anne says. Local authority funds can also really help students with specific disabilities in developing the skills needed to meet the assessment criteria related to written assignments.

CARMEL, DISABILITY ADVISOR
"Lots of students have reported difficulties with addressing the question, particularly those with specific learning difficulties such as dyslexia (1) and dyspraxia (2)"
"One student said that the way the questions were worded was deliberately difficult and that the tutors had gone out of their way to make it difficult for him to understand. I reassured him that this wasn't the case, but that was his perception of it."

(1) 'Dyslexia causes difficulties in learning to read, write and spell. Short-term memory, mathematics, concentration, personal organisation and sequencing may also be affected. ... Dyslexia can occur at any level of intellectual ability. It is not the result of poor motivation, emotional disturbance, sensory impairment or lack of opportunities, but it may occur alongside any of these. The effects of dyslexia can be largely overcome by skilled specialist teaching and the use of compensatory strategies.' The Dyslexia Institute (2002) http://www.dyslexia-inst.org.uk/faqs.htm [accessed 14.08.2006].
(2) 'Dyspraxia is generally recognized to be an impairment or immaturity of the organization of movement. Associated with this may be problems of language, perception and thought.' The Dyspraxia Foundation (2006) http://www.dyspraxiafoundation.org.uk/services/dys_dyspraxia.php [accessed 14.08.2006].

HAWA, DISABILITY ADVISOR

"If a student has quite a severe difficulty in that area, whether or not they have been diagnosed with dyslexia, we can recommend that they see study support tutors and they can sit down with them and receive one-to-one support."

....

JANE, DISABILITY ADVISOR

"We do allow for a variety of different ways of students tackling the question so that they don't have to just sit there and write with pen and paper. Some students find it easier to work at a computer, and if they go for that option then they have the facility for cutting and pasting."

....

JANE COMMENTS

"Well, anything could be a barrier right from being able to get into the library if you are a wheelchair user. Someone with a visual impairment might have difficulties accessing information. If a tutor's using a lot of slides, someone else may find that a good way of accessing information."

Structuring the answer

This is a big issue for many students, and not just those with disabilities, as we have discussed in previous chapters. However, for students who have dyslexia or learning difficulties around grammar and planning, this criterion is even more challenging. Hawa, a disability advisor, comments.

You might also be wondering how you will cope with structuring your answer in exams. The use of computers in exams can be a real boon for students with writing difficulties, as it allows them to correct their mistakes by cutting and pasting and then looking at what they have written on the computer screen. This really helps with the structuring of an essay. Jane, a disability advisor, comments.

Developing understanding

This area is a much more complicated one. There are all sorts of reasons why someone might have problems with developing understanding and it could be argued that this area is not specific to students with special needs. However, certain disabilities might affect how a student actually accesses information in the first place as Jane also comments on.

The issue for many students with disabilities is: 'How can I get around the problem and develop my understanding?'. Most tutors are 'disability aware' and are pro-active in finding alternative ways of disseminating information. If you have a disability and your tutors are not aware of it, the best thing to do is to tell them that you struggle to understand their lectures or the information they are giving you, and then they can ask you about what is the best way to help you. It is important to be persistent about this, as sometimes tutors do not always understand the exact nature of your difficulty or your needs – ask your disability advisor for support if necessary. You're not being awkward; it's your right to seek this help. Hawa offers this advice.

As we mentioned earlier, there are funds available from your local authority if you have difficulties in accessing material that will aid your understanding. Jane explains this in relation to a specific disability. [Continued overleaf →]

HAWA OFFERS ADVICE
"I think the only way to go is to provide the information in a variety of different formats and media, so the learner can use the one that best suits them. That could potentially be a burden on staff, but if you have got systems like a Virtual Learning Environment in place, like we have, then a lot of staff have got into a routine of putting stuff onto the system, which is wonderful for disabled students."

JANE EXPLAINS HOW LOCAL AUTHORITY FUNDS MAY HELP
"Someone with a visual impairment might need some very specialist technology and human support as well, which you couldn't expect the individual tutor to provide."

Developing argument

So far we have looked at specific learning disabilities such as dyslexia, but Hawa, a disability advisor, pointed out that some other groups of students are at a disadvantage when thinking about how to develop an argument in their writing.

Developing argument is a very difficult area within Higher Education and, as we have discussed in previous chapters, many people struggle with it. Hawa also comments on what she advises students to do.

Getting help with developing arguments in your essays is a very good idea, particularly if you have a special learning need or if you fall into that category of students who, while not having a learning disability, come from an educational background which makes it particularly hard to adjust to the demands of university education. If you make an attempt at writing your essay first and then take it to your university's learning support centre, staff should be able to have a look at it with you and make suggestions about ways you could improve it.

....

HAWA, DISABILITY ADVISOR, ON DEVELOPING ARGUMENT
"I suspect that quite a lot of the students that come to us have difficulty with this not because of a disability but because of their previous educational experiences. We get quite a lot of mature students, whose education has not been of a standard format, like A levels etc, and it can be quite difficult for those students to learn what is expected of them in Higher Education."
"I think that all students probably need support with that. Our learning support centre is doing a fantastic job with helping students. We refer many students there."

....

JANE ON E-BOOKS' USES
"They are very useful for a variety of disabled students. Dyslexic students can access information and because it is electronic, they can get their software to read it aloud to them."

Use of evidence

We have looked at the associated problems that students with disabilities have with accessing or finding information to use in their essays. Jane, a disability advisor, recommends e-books to some students.

E-books are electronic versions of books that can be read on a computer and are usually viewed online or downloaded from the internet. Text can also be searched automatically, and cross-referenced using hyperlinks. They can also be a real help to disabled students who have problems getting to the library. Jane comments on other groups of students who could benefit from e-books.

However, there is a word of caution to offer here. The potential difficulty with e-books is that you can cut and paste and there is a great temptation to do that. If you do this, there is a danger that you may fall foul of committing plagiarism and thus fail your essay. The skill is to use the information you read wisely, but if you are having problems with re-writing what you read into your own words, seek some help from your disability advisor or learning support centre.

Evaluation

This criterion is the one that is probably the most difficult of all, so for students with special needs, all the advice earlier in this chapter applies. It is about seeking all the help you can get and being pro-active in getting others, perhaps your fellow students, to help you develop a more critical approach.

JANE ON THOSE WHO MAY BENEFIT FROM E-BOOKS
"Students with visual impairments might be able to enlarge the text on the screen with e-books. Students with mental health difficulties find them useful, as some of them might not be able to get into the library, for example, if they are very nervous in crowded environments."

Students With Special Needs
Action Points

→ If you have a disability or special need, make sure you contact your university's disability support centre. Remember, this is not asking for favours; this is your right, and every university has an obligation to ensure you are not disadvantaged by your disability.

→ If you think you are struggling with written assignments much more than your fellow students, and you are feeling unsure about whether or not you might have a special learning need, make an appointment to discuss your difficulties with a disability advisor. This person is there to help and can give you expert advice. It might be simply a study skills problem, or it might be something that does warrant additional support.

→ Be pro-active and take charge of your learning needs.

Quiz Answers

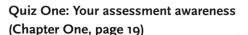

**Quiz One: Your assessment awareness
(Chapter One, page 19)**

1 | **The marks you get for an essay range from 0 – 100**
— FALSE. Although there are differences between
subjects in the range of marks used, most subjects
use a limited range from 35% to 85%.
Advice: The higher up the marking scale you go,
the harder it is to get those extra marks. This is worth
remembering when you have several essays to do at
once or when you are in an examination situation. As
the maths will tell you, it's better to work towards doing
three good essays (60% each) than one outstanding essay
(85%), the latter of which is extremely difficult to achieve
and takes up all your time and effort, leaving you to hurry
and produce two rather poor essays (40% and 45%).
The first strategy gives you an overall average mark of
60%, the second an overall average of 57%.

2 | **A pass mark is always 50%** — FALSE.
A pass mark in most subjects is 40%, sometimes 38%.
Advice: Knowing this might give you some reassurance
if you are feeling overwhelmed by those first university
assignments. Getting 40% is achievable if you are
prepared to do some work, even if you are finding the
subject difficult.

3 | **If you fail an assignment in your first year, this will
affect your final degree** — FALSE **(in most but not all
universities).** Provided you gain 40% overall you will be
allowed to progress into your second year, but the marks
you achieve in this first year will not count towards your
eventual degree classification.
Advice: Universities recognise that it takes a while for

students to learn how to study and perform effectively; therefore, all you have to do is pass your first year overall. The marks you gain will have no effect on your degree classification. This means you can use your first year to experiment a little with what works for you and gets you higher marks and what does not work so well. This in effect is what Lorraine was doing, although she was 'gambling' to a certain extent as she gained her insights only in the second year. You may hear from other students that there's no point in working hard in your first year as it doesn't count. This is an understandable reaction, but it can mean that in the second year such students have a real struggle to meet the much harder requirements. Use your first year wisely to learn how to write good essays.

4 | **Tutors vary in what they expect of you in written essays** — TRUE. In an interview study we carried out with 22 Psychology tutors at two universities (Norton et al., 2004), we found that while all of them used similar assessment criteria, each individual had her or his own 'preferences' for what makes a good essay.
Advice: This is a hard fact to come to grips with and one that may seem immensely frustrating when you're wrestling with what is required, but it's all part and parcel of becoming a skilled writer and developing an awareness of your audience (ie, the person who will be reading and marking your work). Ultimately, this is an essential part of the writing process, as it will help you become progressively more skilful in assessing and evaluating the worth of your own work.

*5 | **It's important to write in as elaborate a style as you can** — FALSE. This is a commonly held belief among students (something we have called a 'rule of the game'; see below), but writing in an over-elaborate style can be an attempt to mask the fact that you don't really understand what it is you are writing about, which leads to taking refuge in rather stilted and pompous phrases.

Advice: It is essential when writing essays to communicate effectively. If your tutor can't understand what you are trying to say, she or he can't give you credit for it. This is why over-elaboration is the enemy of effective writing.

*6 | Handing in an essay before it's due will impress your tutor, who will give you a higher mark — FALSE. This is another 'rule of the game'.

Advice: Handing work in early might be advantageous to you especially if you have several assignments due at about the same time, but it will not automatically earn you higher marks.

*7 | Exceeding the word limit and using big words or technical jargon will get you higher marks — FALSE. This particular 'rule of the game' may sometimes lose you marks.

Advice: This is another example of a strategy students sometimes use when they don't really understand what they are writing about. The danger is that by using big words and/or technical jargon, they may be sticking too closely to someone else's words, which is regarded as plagiarism. The only way to be certain that you are not doing this is to put things into your own words. That way you will be sure that you are not plagiarising, and furthermore it will clearly demonstrate your understanding of the essay topic.

8 | Students in their first year do not generally under-

stand what assessment criteria are — TRUE. Much of
what you read in Chapter Two will show you how many
of the students we interviewed did not really understand
what assessment criteria were and how little they were
aware of how important the criteria were in determining
how well they would do in their essays.

Advice: To give you a head start, we have designed this
book, which we hope will help you not just in your first
year, but also throughout your entire time at university.

9 | **Tutors sometimes give new students higher marks
than their work deserves, to encourage them — TRUE.**
Some, but not all tutors will do this.

Advice: It might reassure you to know that many of your
tutors realise what a difficult task writing an academic
essay at degree level is, and it can be a reminder to you
that the first year is a time for trial and experimentation.
Equally importantly, standards are raised from the first
year to the second year, so you also have to raise the
stakes. Lorraine realised this in her diary.

10 | **Tutors reward ability more than effort — FALSE.**
In a study by Norton et al. (1999) which asked third-year
Psychology students what they thought would be most
rewarded, students thought that ability would be
rewarded more than effort. However, we found that
tutors rewarded effort and ability almost equally.

Advice: This is an encouraging piece of research as it
shows that putting in effort when writing your essays
pays off as much as being 'clever' or grasping difficult
concepts easily.

11 | **Most students think essays are the fairest form of
assessment — TRUE.** In a research study looking at what

students thought were fair ways of assessing (Brunas-Wagstaff & Norton, 1998), essays were seen as the fairest and peer-assessed student presentations as the least fair type of assessment (even more unfair than exams).

Advice: This too is an encouraging piece of information, for it means that however hard the struggle might be to learn how to write effectively, it will pay off, as essay assignments are acknowledged as a fair way of assessing your abilities and understanding.

12 | **A really good student can complete a top-class essay in one sitting** — FALSE. This is one of the myths of the 'super student'. In reality, all essays require a number of drafts, and never more so than an essay which gets a first class mark (70% and above).

Advice: It pays well to allow yourself enough time to write several drafts of an essay (although bear in mind the advice above about not spending too much time and energy on any one assignment at the expense of others). Ideally, if you can give yourself enough time to put the finished essay to one side for a day or two and then look at it with a fresh eye, you will be able to be much more objective and critical than if you were simply to read it through immediately after finishing it.

* All starred items have been taken from a questionnaire that was used in a research study called 'Rules of the Game' (Norton et al., 1996 a, b). This phrase was used to define any tactic that students used in order to impress their tutor and hopefully persuade her or him to give the essay a higher mark than it really deserved. Rules of the Game are not messages from the tutor; they are beliefs that students have generated themselves and are widely believed (by students) to be true. Our research found these were prevalent among a variety of

students. However, tutors did not actually reward students by giving them higher marks for using these tactics. So, devoting time and energy to superficial things that you think might impress your tutor is not a good idea. If you want to read more about this actual research or any of the other research we have done on assessment, see the References on page 122.

Quiz One: Your assessment awareness
Score Interpretation

Score of 9 – 12: Assessment *Orientated*

Well done! You are likely to be a student who knows a lot about how assessment systems work, and you will be keen to find out more. This book points you in directions that will help you develop your academic writing.

Score of 5 – 8: Assessment *Aware*

You fall in the middle category, where you look out for clues about assessment but tend not to seek information about how to write better assignments or take much notice of feedback. You could learn a lot from this book, but you need to apply it to your own work.

Score of 0 – 4: Assessment *Unaware*

A low score on this quiz might indicate that you have never really thought much about assessment before, and that you tend to see it as something done to you which you can't influence in any way. You write your essay, get your mark and don't think too much about how you can do better next time. Hopefully, this book will show you how much you can do to become a better essay writer and get higher marks.

(Note: This is a light-hearted quiz, not a psychological test!)

Quiz Two: Ranking assessment criteria
(Chapter One, page 21)

In the left-hand column of the table of answers below are the rankings of the six tutors who took part in the original study. In the right-hand column are those criteria we describe as 'core', by which we mean assessment criteria that appear frequently and are common across disciplines and institutions. Although different tutors may use slightly different terminology, and each criterion will be interpreted within the context of a specific discipline, the criteria will be recognised by all as referring to fundamental aspects of a good student essay (Elander, et al., 2004).

Rank	Assessment criteria	Core criterion?
2	Understanding	✓
8	Wide reading	
9	English / Spelling	
4	Relevant information	✓
1	Answers the question	✓
6 =	Evaluation	✓
6 =	Presentation / Style	✓
3	Argument	✓
5	Structure / Organisation	✓

Quiz Two: Ranking assessment criteria
Score Interpretation

1 | Answers the question

This was the most important assessment criterion according to the tutors, and, not surprisingly, it is also recognised as a core criterion. Here you can see that the single most important thing you can do in an essay is to answer the question. It sounds simple and straight-forward, doesn't it? But you would be amazed at how easy it is to lose sight of the question when you are doing an extended piece of writing. To find out more about answering the question (sometimes this is known as addressing the question, but the meaning is the same), go to Chapter Four.

2 | Understanding

Think for a minute or two why this is considered to be so important in your essays. Your tutors do not want you to regurgitate information given in lectures or obtained from your reading, as that would be a surface and sterile exercise. Instead, they want you to show in your work that you understand the concepts you are writing about, and that is why this too is considered a core criterion. Chapter Six tells you more.

3 | Argument

This has a particular meaning in Higher Education and is highly valued in academic essays. Nearly all essay titles require some sort of logical developed response, and this is what is meant by developing an argument. This core criterion is the third most important assessment criterion because it is about presenting a well-defended position, something many regard as the hallmark of an academic essay. Presenting an argument means looking at the evidence on both sides of an issue and building a case that is reasoned and balanced and which leads logically to your conclusion. Go to Chapter Seven if you want further information about how to develop an academic argument.

4 | Relevant information

This criterion is more usually known as 'use of evidence' and is quite crucial in all essays in the sciences and social sciences; hence it is another of the 'core' criteria. Basically it means supporting your arguments with reference to other sources. What counts as appropriate evidence varies to some degree between subjects, but generally students writing essays in subjects with a tradition of empirical research should concentrate on empirical research findings reported in journals and on conceptual and theoretical books and papers. See Chapter Eight for more information about the use of evidence.

5 | Structure / Organisation

This was rated as the fifth most important assessment criterion in our study, and it also featured as a core criterion. It is very closely related to answering the question and developing an argument. This is because how you structure your essay determines how well these other criteria are demonstrated. A good structure means more than an introduction, main body and conclusion. It needs to have 'sign-posting' between paragraphs so that your reader knows what point you are making and when you are moving from one point in your argument to another. The structure of your essay should support your considered conclusion. For further advice, see Chapter Five.

6 = | Evaluation

This criterion was originally ranked as sixth, equal with the criterion of Presentation/Style, which we will look at below. Evaluation is sometimes referred to as 'critical evaluation' and is the criterion that tends to separate the 'excellent' from the 'good' or the 'competent' essay. It involves judging the quality and value of what you are reading and incorporating in your essays, and it can present quite a difficult challenge, particularly early in your studies. Chapter Nine gives further information.

6 = | Presentation / Style

This is the other criterion ranked sixth, and it is an interesting one. We have called it core as nearly all tutors mention it as a crucial aspect of writing good essays. You might therefore be surprised to see that it is not featured in this guide. The reason for this is quite simple. Developing an effective written style is considered such an important part of Higher Education generally that most universities offer specialised advice and support, and there are already a number of excellent books and websites dedicated to this; see Further Resources.

8 | Wide reading

You might be surprised to see this assessment criterion so low in the tutors' ranking and that it is not described as a core criterion. The reason for this is that wide reading is seen as an essential part of the core criteria of using evidence, developing an argument and developing your understanding, so it underpins all of these rather than stands alone. See Chapters Six, Seven and Eight.

9 | English / Spelling

This last criterion is another example of something that is already a core criterion, namely, Presentation / Style, as both of these are part of the art of writing well.
See Further Resources.

Quiz Three: Spot the referencing mistakes
(Chapter Eight, page 84)

Errors in the text

Hornby – no date presented.

Gibbs – no first name; surname and date only.

Scouller – no details of source required in the text; surname and date only.

Errors in the list of references

Biggs – the wrong reference has been presented; it should be:

Biggs, J. (2002). Aligning the curriculum to promote good learning. Paper presented at the Constructive Alignment in Action: Imaginative Curriculum Symposium, LTSN Generic Centre, November 2002. Available online at: www.ltsn.ac.uk.

Gibbs – the reference is not presented despite being cited in the text. *This is the major error.*

Gibbs, G. (1999). Using assessment strategically to change the way students learn. In S. Brown & A. Glasner (Eds.), *Assessment Matters in Higher Education.* Buckingham: SRHE & Open University Press. pp 41-53.

Scouller – the full details of the source should be presented here, not in the text:

Scouller, K.M. (1998). The influence of assessment method on students' learning approaches: multiple choice question examination versus assignment essay. *Higher Education*, 35, 453-472.

References and Further Resources

References

Brunas-Wagstaff, J. & Norton, L. (1998). Perceptions of justice in assessment: a neglected factor in improving students as learners. In C. Rust (Ed.), *Improving Student Learning: Improving Students as Learners.* Oxford: The Oxford Centre for Staff and Learning Development. pp. 322-32.

Elander, J., Harrington, K., Norton, L., Robinson, H., Reddy, P., & Stevens, D. (2004). Core assessment criteria for student writing and their implications for supporting student learning. In C. Rust (Ed.), *Improving Student Learning: Theory, Research and Scholarship.* Oxford: The Oxford Centre for Staff and Learning Development. pp. 200-212.

Norton, L.S. (1990). Essay writing: What really counts? *Higher Education*, 20 (4), 411-442.

Norton, L.S., Brunas-Wagstaff, J., & Lockley, S. (1999). Learning outcomes in the traditional coursework essay: Do students and tutors agree? In C. Rust (Ed.), *Improving Student Learning: Improving Student Learning Outcomes.* Oxford: The Oxford Centre for Staff and Learning Development. pp. 240-248.

Norton, L.S., Dickins, T.E., & McLaughlin Cook, A.N.
(1996a). Rules of the Game in essay writing. *Psychology
Teaching Review*, 5, 1, 1-14.

Norton, L.S., Dickins, T.E. & McLaughlin Cook, A.N.
(1996b). Coursework assessment: What are tutors really
looking for? In G. Gibbs (Ed.), *Improving Student
Learning: Using Research to Improve Student Learning*.
Oxford: The Oxford Centre for Staff Development.
pp. 155-166.

Norton, L.S., Ward-Robinson, H., Reddy, P., Elander, J., &
Harrington, K. (2004). Exploring psychology tutors'
views on assessment criteria. Psychology Learning and
Teaching Conference (PLAT 2004), University of
Strathclyde, 5-7 April 2004. (Paper available from the
first author).

Stephenson, J. (1998). The concept of capability and its
importance in higher education. In J. Stephenson & M.
Yorke (Eds.), *Capability and Quality in Higher Education*.
London: Kogan Page. pp. 1-13.

Further Resources – Books

Clanchy, J. (1997). *Essay writing for students: a practical guide.* Melbourne: Addison Wesley Longman.

Creme, P. & Lea, M.R. (1997). *Writing at university: a guide for students,* 2nd ed. Buckingham: Open University.

Fairbairn, G.J. & Fairbairn, S. (2001). *Reading at University: A Guide for Students.* Buckingham: Open University.

Fairbairn, G.J. & Winch, C. (1996). *Reading, Writing and Reasoning: A Guide for Students.* Buckingham: Open University.

Hennessy, B. (2002). *Writing an Essay: Simple Techniques to Transform Your Coursework and Examinations (Student Handbooks).* Oxford: How To Books.

Levin, P. (2004). *Write Great Essays! Reading and Essay Writing for Undergraduates and Taught Postgraduates.* Buckingham: Open University.

Redman, P. (2001). *Good Essay Writing: a Social Sciences Guide.* London: Sage.

Turley, R.M. (2000). *Writing Essays: A Guide for Students in English and the Humanities.* London: Routledge.

Further Resources – Websites

http://www.open.ac.uk/study-strategies/
The Open University's general advice on writing
and assessment

http://dissc.tees.ac.uk/
The University of Teesside's wide range of advice
on essays, exams, academic writing and plagiarism

http://www.rlf.org.uk/fellowshipscheme/writing/
essayguide.cfm
The Royal Literary Fund's essay writing advice

http://www.uefap.com/vocab/vocfram.htm
A guide to using English for academic purposes

http://www.ioe.ac.uk/caplits/writingcentre/index.htm
The Institute of Education's advice on writing essays,
reports, critical reviews and dissertations

Acknowledgments

This book is the result of a collaborative endeavour of a number of colleagues, past and present, who have worked on the HEFCE-funded Assessment Plus consortium project led by London Metropolitan University with partner institutions Liverpool Hope University and Aston University. For further information and details on this project, please see the website: http://www.writenow.ac.uk/assessmentplus.

Thanks to Guenter A Plum (http://functionaledit.com) for a thorough proofreading job. This book would also not have been possible without the time given up to be interviewed by so many students, tutors and disability advisors and their willingness to allow their experiences to be shared in this way. We are very grateful to each and every one of them.